• T R O P H I E S •

Language Handbook

Grade 6

Printed in the United States of America

ISBN 0-15-325068-2

10 073 10 09 08 07 06

Orlando   Boston   Dallas   Chicago   San Diego

Visit *The Learning Site!*
www.harcourtschool.com

CONTENTS

Visit *The Learning Site!*
www.harcourtschool.com

Grammar, Usage, and Mechanics   103

(Includes Cumulative Reviews)

Sentences

Contents

Your Best Writing

Writing is a way of sharing your ideas. Of course, you share ideas when you talk with others, too. When you write, however, you end up with a lasting record. Writing captures your thoughts just as a photograph captures your appearance.

This *Language Handbook* will help you put your thoughts into writing. It will give you the skills, strategies, tips, and models you need to write easily and effectively. Let's start with an introduction to the writing process and some ongoing strategies.

The Writing Process

One big difference between writing and talking is the element of time. When you write, you have time to plan what you'll say, say it, and then make changes until it's just right. This is your writing process. Though there is no one correct way to write, many writers go through the stages shown at right.

Prewriting

In this stage, you prepare to write. You plan what you will write by choosing a topic, identifying your audience, brainstorming and researching ideas, and organizing information.

Drafting

Next you follow your prewriting plan to express your ideas in a first draft. Don't expect perfection—just let the sentences flow according to your plan.

Revising

Now you have the opportunity to improve your writing. As you edit, you will look for ways to clarify or enrich what you have written. You might edit by yourself or ask others for input to see how well your writing communicates.

Proofreading

Mistakes can confuse your readers and distract them from your ideas. In this final stage of editing, you check for errors in grammar, spelling, capitalization, and punctuation. Then you make a clean, final copy.

Publishing

Now it's time to choose a way to share your writing with your audience. You might create a newsletter or pamphlet, present an oral reading, mail a letter, or assemble a class book.

Keeping a Writer's Journal

Many writers use a journal to jot down ideas for writing. You can use a journal to record special observations, take notes on what you learn, and try out different forms of writing. The only limit is your imagination.

First, choose a notebook you like. Decorate the cover if you wish. Then begin to fill the pages with your ideas.

Set aside a section of your journal to be a **Word Bank**. This is a place to keep track of new, useful, or interesting vocabulary words. Your Word Bank might include words you discover while reading or while learning a new sport or activity. Create categories for your words, such as music words, words from other languages, strong verbs, and vivid adjectives. When you are writing, you can visit your Word Bank for inspiration.

Reading ↔ Writing Connection

Reading other people's writing can help you learn to evaluate your own work. Take time to think about the quality of the writing whenever you read an article, ad, letter, or brochure. Do you think the writing is clear? What is the writer trying to communicate?

Keeping a Portfolio

A photo album is a collection of photographs that records cherished memories. In an effective album, the photos are carefully selected and organized. You can collect and organize your written work in a portfolio.

You may want to create two different kinds of portfolios. A **working portfolio** includes works-in-progress or unfinished ideas. A **show portfolio** includes the finished writing that you want to share with others. You might organize your show portfolio by date of composition or by type of writing, such as fiction, nonfiction, or letters.

Both portfolios will be useful during a writing conference with your teacher. Use the work in each portfolio to review your accomplishments and your growth as a writer. Your best work will indicate your strongest writing skills. Less effective samples may point to skills you can improve.

Writer's Craft and Writing Traits

You've probably heard the phrase "arts and crafts" used to describe handmade items like quilts or pottery. Craftspeople make works of art that are both creative and useful. You can think of writing as a craft, too. Instead of using clay to make a bowl, you use words to build an essay, a letter, or a poem.

A key part of developing your craft is recognizing good writing. A potter might look for a symmetrical shape and thin, even edges. This web shows some of the traits you should look for in a piece of writing.

The Traits of Good Writing

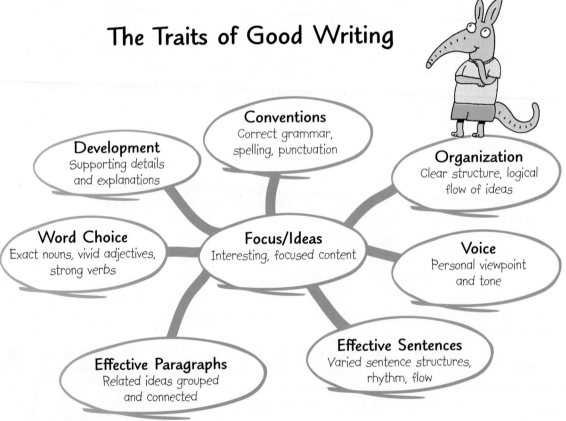

Conventions
Correct grammar, spelling, punctuation

Development
Supporting details and explanations

Organization
Clear structure, logical flow of ideas

Word Choice
Exact nouns, vivid adjectives, strong verbs

Focus/Ideas
Interesting, focused content

Voice
Personal viewpoint and tone

Effective Paragraphs
Related ideas grouped and connected

Effective Sentences
Varied sentence structures, rhythm, flow

Traits Checklist

Questions like these can help you improve your skills. Every time you answer "yes" to one of these questions, you recognize a strength of your writing.

☑ **FOCUS/IDEAS**	Is my writing clear and focused? Do I keep my purpose and audience in mind?
☑ **ORGANIZATION**	Do my ideas have a logical flow? Is my beginning effective? What about my ending?
☑ **DEVELOPMENT**	Have I supported my ideas with interesting details and reasons?
☑ **VOICE**	Does the writing sound like I wrote it? Have I added personal touches and shown that I care about what I am saying?
☑ **EFFECTIVE SENTENCES**	Do I use different kinds of sentences? Do I use the best sentence structure for my ideas?
☑ **EFFECTIVE PARAGRAPHS**	Does each paragraph focus on one idea? Do I use transitions to tie ideas together?
☑ **WORD CHOICE**	Do I use energetic words that create interest? Have I used strong verbs, precise nouns, and vivid adjectives?
☑ **CONVENTIONS**	Are my grammar, spelling, and punctuation correct?

Try This! Use the checklist to review an example of your writing. What traits of good writing do you find in your work? Which areas could be improved?

Focus/Ideas

An article or story that doesn't have a clear focus is vague or confusing. It might jump around from topic to topic. You can learn to avoid vague writing. Find a focus and stick with it. Determine the main idea you want to write about. Then choose details that support the main idea.

Do you ever have trouble thinking of ideas? Most writers do. Keeping track of your experiences in your Writer's Journal is a good way to collect ideas for writing. Drawing, looking at photos, or talking to someone can also help you get ideas.

Here is one student's informational paragraph. Think about how the writer stays focused on a main idea.

Student Model

The common barn owl actually has several unusual features. This owl has a curious face. The eyes and beak are surrounded by a heart-shaped ruff of white feathers. It has no tufts around its ears. The barn owl also makes an odd sound. Most owls hoot. The call of the barn owl sounds more like a scratchy hiss. You should be able to identify a barn owl if you can see its face or hear its call.

A topic sentence states the main idea.

What details support the main idea?

How does the final sentence summarize the paragraph?

Try This! Suppose that you have been asked to write an article for your school newspaper about the history of your school. Name three ways that you could get ideas for the article.

How to Focus Your Writing

Strategies	Examples
Narrow your topic.	Narrow the topic "earthquakes" to "How to Prepare for an Earthquake" or "My Earthquake Experience."
Remember your purpose and audience.	If you are writing an informational report, focus on facts and use a formal style and tone. If you are writing a story for children, keep the words and ideas simple and entertaining.
Stick to your topic.	If you are writing about preparing for earthquakes at home, don't include details about what causes earthquakes or how you like your house.

Reading ↔ Writing Connection

Two pieces of writing that have the same topic might still have different focuses. Read two magazine articles about the same topic. Compare and contrast the focuses of the two articles.

Focus/Ideas

Follow these steps to write an informational report with a clear focus.

Writing Prompt

Write an informational report for readers your age that focuses on an endangered animal. Learn more about your topic by using textbooks, encyclopedias, and online resources.

Prewrite

As you gather information, make an informal outline to plan your report.

Topic/Main idea

Subtopic

Subtopic

Subtopic

Conclusion

Draft

Follow these steps to organize your report.

STEP 1 **Introduce the topic.** Write an interesting opening paragraph that states your main idea.

STEP 2 **Organize the subtopics.** Write one paragraph for each subtopic.

STEP 3 **Add supporting facts and details**. Give facts and details that support each subtopic.

STEP 4 **Conclude with a summary.** In your last paragraph, summarize your main points.

Strategies Good Writers Use

- Think about what will keep your reader's interest. You might even imagine that your ideal reader is sitting next to you as you write.
- If you get stuck, try saying what you want to say aloud. Then write it down.

Revise

Use this checklist to help you revise your informational report:

- ☑ Does the topic sentence of each paragraph relate to the main topic of your report?
- ☑ Do all the details in each paragraph relate to the topic?
- ☑ Do you need to add more interesting details?
- ☑ Does the order of ideas make sense?

Proofread

Use this checklist as you proofread your report:

- ☑ Have you used capitalization and punctuation correctly?
- ☑ Have you indented the first line of each paragraph?
- ☑ Have you used singular and plural nouns correctly?
- ☑ Have you used a dictionary to check your spelling?

 delete text

 insert text

↻ move text

¶ new paragraph

≡ capitalize

/ lowercase

◯ correct spelling

Publish and Reflect

Turn your report into a brochure. Add artwork or photographs. After classmates have read your brochure, discuss it with them. What did they learn from your report? Write your reflections in your Writer's Journal.

Organization

There are many ways of organizing writing. **Time order** is used most often to describe an event or a process. Other descriptions work well using **spatial order;** you might describe what you see from left to right or top to bottom. In persuasive writing, you can use **order of importance**, to organize your reasons from least to most important. In expository writing, ideas are often grouped in **categories,** such as likes and dislikes or similarities and differences. Whatever organization you choose, **transition words,** such as *first, then,* and *similarly*, help the reader to follow your ideas.

The paragraphs below are from a student's comparison-and-contrast essay about choosing a dog mascot for his school's end-of-the-year party. As you read, think about how the ideas are organized.

Student Model

Who will be our "Dog Days Dog" this year—Couch Potato Pete or Moxie Maxie? Before you decide, consider the facts. Both dogs are setters, so either one could set the mood for our "Dog Days" party. Both dogs love people, and neither one of them barks much.

The dogs look different, however. Couch Potato Pete is a black and white dog, but Maxie has a red coat. The dogs behave differently, too. Couch Potato Pete's favorite activity is sitting around watching TV. Maxie, in contrast, loves to run and play.

The writer uses a question to grab the reader's interest and introduce the topic.

How does the writer group the ideas into paragraphs?

Notice the transition words *however, too,* and *in contrast.*

How to Organize Information

Organizational Patterns	Uses	Transition Words
Time order	narratives, stories (may include flashbacks), how-to explanations, reports on historical events	after, before, finally, first, last, later, next, now, soon, then, at the same time
Spatial order	descriptions, directions	to begin with, first, above, across from, around, below, here, inside, next to, over, there, under
Order of importance	persuasive essays, with the most important reason first or last; friendly letters, with the most important news first	above all, first, last, primarily, second, third, most important
Categories	writing about advantages and disadvantages, likes and dislikes, causes and effects, similarities and differences	both, also, another, in the same way, in contrast, on the other hand, as a result

Organization

Follow these suggestions to write a comparison-and-contrast essay.

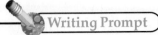
Writing Prompt

Write an essay in which you compare and contrast two places, such as two houses you have lived in, or two schools you have attended.

Prewrite

Use a Venn diagram to organize your topic.

> **Strategies**
> **Good Writers Use**
>
> • Choose an organizational pattern that fits your topic.
> • Compare and contrast specific points, such as size and atmosphere.
> • Include your opinions as well as factual details when writing an essay.

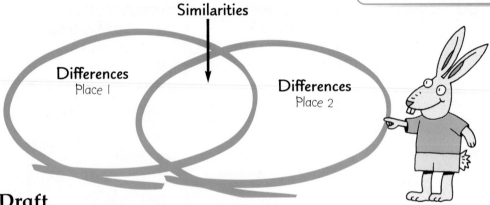

Similarities

Differences
Place 1

Differences
Place 2

Draft

Use these steps to write your first draft.

STEP 1 **Introduce the topic.** Name what you are comparing and contrasting, and give background information.

STEP 2 **Group similarities and differences.** Decide whether to put similarities or differences first. Write a paragraph about each. Use transitions to move from point to point.

STEP 3 **Write a conclusion.** End with a summary or a judgment.

Revise

Review your draft. Use this checklist to help you revise your writing:

- ☑ Is the introduction of your topic clear?
- ☑ Are the similarities and differences grouped logically?
- ☑ Does each paragraph have a topic sentence?
- ☑ Did you include facts and examples in each body paragraph?
- ☑ Did you use transition words to connect your ideas?

Proofread

Use this checklist as you proofread your essay:

- ☑ Have you used capitalization and punctuation correctly?
- ☑ Have you distinguished between possessive nouns and plural nouns?
- ☑ Have you not shifted verb tense unnecessarily?
- ☑ Have you used a dictionary to check your spelling?

ℓ	delete text
∧	insert text
∽	move text
¶	new paragraph
≡	capitalize
/	lowercase
◯	correct spelling

Publish and Reflect

Make a final copy of your essay and then read it aloud to classmates. What do your listeners' questions show about their understanding of your essay? Record your ideas in your Writer's Journal.

Voice

When you write, your **voice** reflects everything from your sense of humor to the ideas you believe. Your voice gives your writing a **tone**, or an attitude toward the subject. Your tone may vary according to what you are writing about. For example, it may be serious or humorous, sympathetic or critical.

Read this descriptive paragraph. Think about how the writer shows his feelings toward his subject.

Student Model

Some of my friends think I'm crazy, but I like baseball better on radio than on television. When I listen to the radio, I get to imagine everything. In my mind, I see the pitcher kicking the pitcher's mound and turning quickly to look at the runners on base who might try to steal. Then he hurls the ball. I see the batter swing and smack the ball into the outfield. If I close my eyes, I can almost smell the thick dust as the runner slides into home. The announcers say what's happening, but the sounds of the game say even more. The crowd roars like a giant dragon when someone hits a home run. Watching baseball on television isn't nearly as much fun because you see only what the camera sees.

The writer establishes his viewpoint.

Descriptive words appeal to the reader's senses and create a feeling of excitement.

The writer concludes with a strong opinion.

Try This! What sport do you most enjoy watching? How does watching this sport appeal to your senses?

How to Develop Your Writing Voice

Strategies	Examples
Use figurative language and imagery. Common types of figurative language are **similes, metaphors,** and **personification.** **Imagery** is vivid language that helps the reader form a mental picture.	The pond's water was a silver mirror. (metaphor comparing water to a mirror) The wind whispered to the falling leaves. (gives wind a human quality) The campfire flickered fitfully in the dark night. (paints a picture with words)
Include sensory details. **Sensory details** appeal to the five senses: sight, hearing, touch, smell, and taste. They help the reader share your experience.	**Sight** and **touch:** The furry black cat slowly stretched before curling up and falling asleep again. **Hearing** and **smell:** The bakery was filled with the heavy pounding of bread being kneaded and the hearty aroma of fresh yeast.
Express a viewpoint and tone. Let your reader know how you feel about the subject. Remember that your viewpoint—the way you look at the subject—makes your writing original.	Choose words and details that suggest emotions, such as joy, curiosity, or dissatisfaction. *Note the difference:* Our lazy mutt flopped on the floor. Our trusty dog waited expectantly.

Voice

Use these steps to write a descriptive paragraph that reflects your personal voice.

Writing Prompt

Choose a scene to describe. It might be scary, funny, or peaceful. Write a descriptive paragraph. Use sensory details that show how you feel about the scene.

Strategies Good Writers Use

- Choose a topic you know firsthand.
- Make an ordinary topic interesting through your use of voice.
- Include specific details that make your viewpoint clear.

Prewrite

In a web, organize words and phrases that describe your topic. Decide on the feeling or mood you want to create.

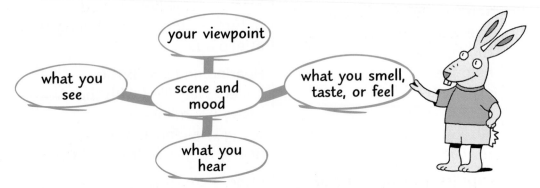

your viewpoint

what you see

scene and mood

what you smell, taste, or feel

what you hear

Draft

Follow these steps to organize your descriptive paragraph:

STEP 1 **Begin with a topic sentence.** Identify the subject of your paragraph.

STEP 2 **Write in your own voice.** Use details and language that tell how you feel about the scene.

STEP 3 **Sum up the experience.** Conclude with a statement that summarizes your viewpoint.

Revise

Review your draft, looking for opportunities to add personal touches. What changes will make your description sharper for your reader? Use this checklist to help you revise your paragraph:

- ☑ Do you include images that will help your reader picture your subject?
- ☑ Can you add figurative language or sensory details to create a stronger impression?
- ☑ Does your writing have a tone?
- ☑ Is your viewpoint clearly reflected?

✐	delete text
∧	insert text
↻	move text
¶	new paragraph
≡	capitalize
/	lowercase
◯	correct spelling

Proofread

Use this checklist as you proofread your paragraph:

- ☑ Have you used correct capitalization and punctuation?
- ☑ Have you used complete sentences, not sentence fragments?
- ☑ Have you used words like *it's* and *its, your* and *you're, their* and *there* correctly?
- ☑ Have you used a dictionary to check your spelling?

Publish and Reflect

Share your description by reading it aloud to a partner. Ask your partner to close his or her eyes and imagine the scene. Then listen to your partner's paragraph. Identify the strongest features of each paragraph. In your journal, jot down ideas for developing your personal voice in future writing projects.

Word Choice

An artist uses rich colors to bring a portrait or a scene to life. When you write, the words you use are your colors. **Vivid words** create strong, clear images in the reader's mind. If you want to describe someone who is happy, instead of using the vague word *happy*, you might write about a *joyful grin*, a *contented smile*, or a *jolly laugh*.

Whether you are creating images or explaining ideas, your writing will be strongest if your words are **exact**, or precise. If you use a thesaurus, keep in mind that synonyms do not have exactly the same meaning.

Read this student's character sketch, and think about how the words and phrases help you understand Mr. Piñol.

Student Model

Mr. Piñol always wore a crisp, white lab coat and began his science class with strict formality. When he took attendance, his voice sounded as flat and rigid as his starched coat.

> Notice the vivid adjectives and the comparison between Mr. Piñol's voice and his coat.

At the start of a lesson, he would try to sound serious, but soon his excitement would take over and break through his stiff appearance. He loved science so much that he couldn't hide his enthusiasm. In no time at all he would begin to dash off energetic sketches or playfully act out chemical reactions.

> What words tell you about Mr. Piñol's real personality?

By the end of class, Mr. Piñol's formality had disappeared. He would unbutton his confining lab coat so that he could move more freely as he led his students deeper into the exciting mysteries of science.

> How does the writer feel about Mr. Piñol? How can you tell?

Strategies for Choosing Words

Strategies	Examples
Use vivid words.	Use verbs like *barks* or *whispers* to tell how a person speaks. Use describing words like *colossal* or *petite*, *briskly* or *sluggishly*, and phrases like *smile as sweet as honey*.
Use exact words.	Use specific nouns like *ship* or *yacht* instead of a general noun like *boat*. Choose the right synonym: Is your idea a *belief* or a *conviction*?
Pay attention to connotations, the positive or negative emotional meanings of words.	Does someone *laugh* or *snicker*? Is the perfume *fragrant* or *smelly*?

Try This! Find a description of a character in a book or story. How does the description lead you to feel about the character? Make a list of words with positive and/or negative connotations in the description. You may want to add some of the words to your Word Bank.

Writing Forms

A character sketch uses vivid words to make the writing expressive and establishes a tone that indicates the author's feelings toward the subject.

For more about character description, see page 65.

Word Choice

Choose the perfect words. Follow these steps to write a character sketch.

Writing Prompt

What do you want to be like as an adult? Write a description of yourself. Use the third-person point of view. You might put yourself in a particular place, such as at work, at home, or at play.

Strategies Good Writers Use

- Show a character in action.
- Use specific details from your imagination.
- Create a central impression of the character.

Prewrite

First, picture yourself as an adult. Then use a web to brainstorm details.

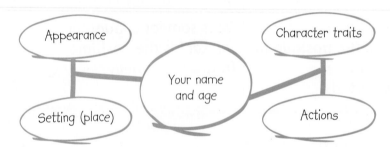

Appearance

Character traits

Your name and age

Setting (place)

Actions

Draft

Follow these steps to draft your character sketch.

STEP 1 **Introduce the topic.** Introduce your adult self in an interesting way. You might use the present tense to tell something the character is doing.

STEP 2 **Provide details.** Use specific details that suggest the character's traits as well as describe appearance.

STEP 3 **Draw a conclusion.** End with a statement that sums up what the character is like.

Revise

Read over the draft of your character sketch. What changes will make your description more effective? Use this checklist to help you revise your work:

☑ Does your description present a clear picture of the way you see yourself as an adult?

☑ Can you replace any words with more exact or vivid words or phrases?

☑ Does your description create a positive feeling about the subject?

☑ Have you avoided the pronoun I and stayed in the third-person point of view?

✐	delete text
∧	insert text
↻	move text
¶	new paragraph
≡	capitalize
/	lowercase
○	correct spelling

Proofread

Use the checklist as you proofread your writing:

☑ Have you capitalized proper nouns?

☑ Have you used the correct form and spelling for irregular verbs?

☑ Have you punctuated sentences correctly?

☑ Have you used a dictionary to correct your spelling?

Publish and Reflect

Make a final copy of your character sketch, and share it with a partner. Point out vivid words and details in each other's work. Share your ideas about how word choice can help you improve your writing. Write your thoughts in your Writer's Journal.

Development

When you write, adding reasons and details to explain your ideas is called **development**. When you are writing to persuade, you need to develop your ideas in order to convince your reader that you are right.

Read this student's persuasive letter. Notice how he uses development to support his ideas and clarify his opinion.

Student Model

Dear Newsbrook Town Council:

I am writing to encourage Newsbrook to install bicycle racks downtown. This plan will benefit both bicyclists and non-riders.

Many people already enjoy bicycling to our town. Unfortunately, there is nowhere for bikes to park. Riders have to lock their bikes to trees or parking meters. By noon, bikes clutter our sidewalks dangerously.

Bike racks would provide a convenient parking place. Cycles would also be out of the way of traffic and pedestrians.

Finally, bike racks would encourage more people to ride bicycles into town, which will reduce both traffic and pollution.

Sincerely,

David Lipovetsky

What is David's opinion?

What facts and details does David provide that support his opinion?

What additional reason does David explain in his closing paragraph?

Try This! Think of a simple plan, like installing bicycle parking racks, that would improve your town or your school. Identify at least two reasons why you think your idea is a good one.

How to Develop Ideas

Strategies	Applying Strategies
• **Identify your purpose and audience.**	• Choose words and ideas that will help you achieve your goal and interest your readers. Be careful not to offend your audience.
• **Use reasons and details.**	• Organize your reasons in an effective order. Often the least important reason is put in the middle. The most important may come first or last. • Support each reason with details, such as facts, examples, and anecdotes (brief stories that illustrate a point).
• **Stay on the topic.**	• Your details should be relevant. Omit any information that wanders off the topic or blurs your focus.

Writing Forms

Persuasive writing offers strong reasons to support an opinion and develops those reasons with facts, details, and examples.

For more about persuasive writing, see pages 84–85.

Development

Now it's your turn to back up one of your own opinions. The following steps will help you write a persuasive essay using reasons and details to support a strong opinion.

Strategies
Good **W**riters **U**se

- Focus on your purpose before you begin writing.
- Consider your audience's background. What reasons are most likely to appeal to them?
- Know your subject well.

Writing Prompt

Write an essay nominating one creative work for a school hall of fame. You might choose a book, movie, or song. Write to convince the students and teachers at your school that your choice deserves their votes. Support your opinion with at least three reasons.

Prewrite

Use a web to develop your ideas.

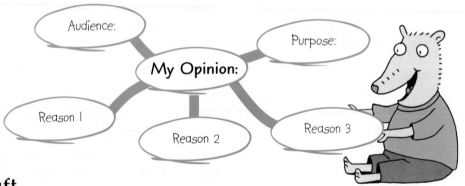

Audience:

Purpose:

My Opinion:

Reason 1

Reason 2

Reason 3

Draft

Follow these steps to draft your essay:

STEP 1 **Grab your audience's attention.** Begin with a catchy statement to get your audience's attention. Then state your opinion clearly and directly.

STEP 2 **Organize and support reasons.** Include three reasons that support your opinion. Organize these in order of importance, with the most important reason last.

STEP 3 **Conclude with a powerful summary.** Restate your opinion in a way that leaves a lasting impression.

Revise

Review your persuasive essay. Can you make any changes that will make it more convincing? Use this checklist to help you revise your work:

- ☑ Is your opinion clearly stated at the beginning of the essay?
- ☑ Does each paragraph explain one reason?
- ☑ Are any of your reasons weakly supported? If so, what details, facts, or examples can you add to make the reasons more persuasive?
- ☑ Have you stayed focused on your topic, audience, and purpose?

℘	delete text
∧	insert text
↻	move text
¶	new paragraph
☰	capitalize
/	lowercase
◯	correct spelling

Proofread

Use this checklist as you proofread your essay:

- ☑ Have you used quotation marks or underlining to punctuate titles correctly?
- ☑ Have you capitalized and punctuated sentences correctly?
- ☑ Have you used a dictionary to check your spelling?
- ☑ Have you indented each paragraph?

Publish and Reflect

Make a final copy of your persuasive essay. Read your essay aloud to the class. You might vote as a class to decide which works will enter the school hall of fame. Then discuss how class writers used development to support their opinions. Record your ideas for improving your writing in your Writer's Journal.

Writer's Journal

Effective Sentences

You are a student. You are learning about writing. You are reading this book. You are probably getting bored of sentences that start with "You are."

Repetitive sentences are dull, and so are bland sentences. Writing the same kind of sentence over and over is a sure way to lose your readers' interest. On the other hand, you'll keep your readers' attention if you write varied and vigorous sentences.

Read the opening of this student's personal narrative. Notice how the writer uses a variety of effective sentences to describe an event from his life.

Student Model

Mom and Dad always say that amazing things happen when you least expect them. I used to think that was just their way of saying "hurry up and wait." Now I know the truth. My parents were right.

While I was working in our community garden, an ancient beast came to say hello. I was digging a hole for a rose bush when I heard a hollow clink. My shovel had hit something. I dug around the object and began to see my prize. I found a rock the size of a toaster, but it was split in two pieces. The first bang of my shovel must have cracked it open. The real treasure was inside. Who would believe that you can find a two-pound prehistoric fossil in a suburban patch of dirt?

> The writer begins with sentences that make you curious about what happened.

> The writer mixes simple, compound, and complex sentences.

> The writer includes a question to add interest.

How to Write Effective Sentences

Strategies	Examples
• **Avoid wordy sentences.** Weed out unnecessary words. Sentences that begin with *There is/There was* often can be tightened.	• There were many students who were wearing green on Saint Patrick's Day. *Tightened:* Many students wore green on Saint Patrick's Day.
• **Combine sentences.** Look for ways to use compound subjects and predicates. Combine simple sentences to create compound and complex sentences.	• We saw the funnel descending from the cloud. We ran for the shelter. *Combined:* When we saw the funnel descending from the cloud, we ran for the shelter.
• **Use different kinds of sentences.** Use statements, questions, commands, and exclamations.	• I felt like Cinderella when her coach turned back into a pumpkin. I never want to have a surprise like that again!

Writing Forms

A personal narrative uses the first-person point of view to tell a story about the author's own experience.

For more about personal narratives, see pages 68–69.

Effective Sentences

Follow these steps to write a personal narrative that uses sentences effectively.

Writing Prompt

Think of a time when you faced a change in your life, such as moving or getting a new family member. Write a personal narrative telling your classmates about the change and how it affected you.

Strategies Good Writers Use

- Keep your purpose and audience in mind. Remember that your audience doesn't know everything you do, so you may need to explain some details from your life.
- Use time order to help readers follow the sequence of events.

Prewrite

Use a flowchart to list the events you will describe.

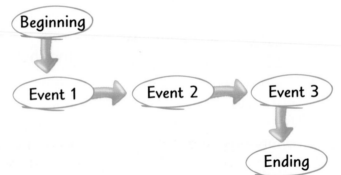

Beginning

Event 1 → Event 2 → Event 3

Ending

Draft

Use these steps to organize your narrative:

STEP 1 **Get your audience's attention.** Begin your narrative with an interesting sentence.

STEP 2 **Write the beginning of your narrative.** Be sure to describe settings or people your readers may be unfamiliar with.

STEP 3 **Write the middle of your narrative.** Continue telling the events in the order in which they happened. Remember to vary your sentences.

STEP 4 **Write the ending.** Conclude by explaining what the events meant to you.

Revise

Read over the draft of your personal narrative. How might you make your sentences—and your narrative—more effective? Use this checklist to help you revise your personal narrative:

☑ Will your opening grab your readers' attention?

☑ Does your writing have an appealing rhythm, using both long and short sentences?

☑ Could you combine some sentences to vary sentence length?

☑ Can you tighten the wording in any of your sentences?

ℓ	delete text
∧	insert text
↻	move text
¶	new paragraph
≡	capitalize
/	lowercase
◯	correct spelling

Proofread

Use this checklist as you proofread your narrative:

☑ Have you used commas correctly in compound sentences?

☑ Have you used commas after introductory dependent clauses?

☑ Have you capitalized proper nouns?

☑ Have you used a dictionary to check your spelling?

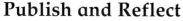

Publish and Reflect

Read your narrative aloud to a partner. You might decide to record your reading and listen to the flow of sentences as you read. Talk with your partner about how effectively your sentences tell your story. Record your thoughts for improving your own writing in your Writer's Journal.

Effective Paragraphs

Writers use paragraphs to shape information or ideas. In nonfiction writing such as essays and reports, each paragraph focuses on a single idea, which is often stated in a topic sentence. The other sentences provide details about the main idea.

Short stories and other kinds of fiction also use paragraphs to group ideas. When the scene changes, an event begins, or a speaker changes, the writer starts a new paragraph.

Read the beginning of this student's short story. Think about why the writer started each new paragraph.

Student Model

Leila had a tough decision to make. Would she go to the mall and get her favorite tennis player's autograph? Or would she spend the time practicing for her own tennis tournament next week?

"There's no right choice," she moaned to her sister, Tasha.

"Maybe there's a happy middle," suggested Tasha. "Can you do both?"

At first Leila just moaned again, assuming her sister's idea was impossible. Then she remembered Grandpa John, who always said, "Nothing is impossible if you try hard enough." Maybe Tasha was on the right track after all.

The first paragraph begins with a topic sentence, which is followed by details explaining it.

The words of a single speaker are contained in a single paragraph. When Tasha responds to Leila, the writer begins a new paragraph.

Why do the sentences in this paragraph belong together?

Strategies for Writing Effective Paragraphs

1. Write an interesting opening paragraph.

The paragraph that introduces an essay or a report is a special kind of paragraph. Introduce your topic with an opening that has an unusual twist or intriguing idea. A short, surprising sentence, a vivid image, or an engaging question can be effective.

2. Write a topic sentence, and give details that relate to it.

Topic sentence: Tasha often helped her younger sister solve problems.

Details: She knew that Leila often ran out of time. So Tasha tried to help Leila set up reasonable schedules.

3. Give information or events in the correct order, or sequence. Use transition words and phrases.

Tasha and Leila talked. <u>After their conversation</u>, Leila made up her mind.

4. Start a new paragraph for each speaker.

You were right," Leila told Tasha. "I had time to get the autograph, study, and practice tennis, too."

"I knew it," said Tasha. "You just needed a plan."

Try This! Choose several lines of dialogue from a play or a comic strip. Then write the dialogue in short story form. For example:

"Wake up, sleepyhead," said Mr. Wilson.

Saundra stretched as she woke up. "Is it morning already?" she asked.

"Morning?" snapped her father. "It's practically tomorrow!"

Effective Paragraphs

Follow these steps to write a short story that uses effective paragraphs.

Writing Prompt

Write a short story about a character who must solve a difficult problem that seems almost impossible. Create a believable story by including sharp details, strong words, and realistic dialogue. Remember to use paragraphs effectively.

Strategies Good Writers Use

- Remember that the purpose of a story is to entertain.
- Write about a problem (and solution) that will interest your audience.
- Brainstorming a list of traits can help you create a lifelike character.

Prewrite

Use a story map to plan your story.

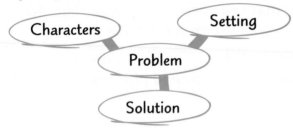

Characters

Setting

Problem

Solution

Draft

Follow these steps to organize your story:

STEP 1 **Introduce the setting and characters.** Begin your story by introducing your main character(s) and establishing the time and place.

STEP 2 **Provide the problem.** Introduce the main character's challenge with a topic sentence that states the problem.

STEP 3 **Solve the problem step by step.** Describe the steps the character takes to solve the problem. Include descriptive details. Use dialogue to move your story along.

STEP 4 **Conclude your story.** In your final paragraph, explain how the characters feel when the problem is solved.

Revise

Read over the draft of your short story. Use this checklist to help you revise your story:

- ☑ Did you tell the story clearly from beginning to end, including all of the steps in between?
- ☑ Does every paragraph focus on one topic, event, or speaker?
- ☑ Have you used transition words to help your reader understand how events are related?
- ☑ Should any of your paragraphs be combined because they focus on the same topic? Should any be divided because the focus is on more than one topic?

ℒ	delete text
∧	insert text
↻	move text
¶	new paragraph
☰	capitalize
/	lowercase
◯	correct spelling

Proofread

Use this checklist as you proofread your story:

- ☑ Have you capitalized proper nouns?
- ☑ Have you indented the first line of each paragraph?
- ☑ Have you used quotation marks and commas correctly when punctuating dialogue?
- ☑ Have you used a dictionary to check your spelling?

Publish and Reflect

Make a final copy of your story. Add illustrations, and place your finished story in a class reading area. In the next few days, read three or four stories by your classmates. After reading each story, jot down in your Writer's Journal any ideas you get for your own writing.

Conventions

Written English follows certain **conventions**, or rules, that make it clear for readers. As you proofread, look for errors in your use of conventions. Once you have revised your writing to improve organization, tone, and word use, you can polish it in the proofreading stage.

Proofreading Strategies

Wait before proofreading. If you can, avoid proofreading your writing immediately. Set your draft aside, and return to it with a fresh eye.

Proofread in stages. You might want to follow these steps:

1. Read your composition for meaning. Notice whether you have indented **paragraphs** and whether your **sentences** make sense. Correct any fragments and run-ons.
2. Next, look at **grammar, usage, capitalization,** and **punctuation**. Think about the rules you have learned, and apply them to your own writing.
3. Last, focus on **spelling**. Take the time to look up any mystery words in a dictionary.

Proofread with a partner. A second set of eyes may see problems that you have overlooked.

Technology

Keep track of your revisions. First, make a copy of your old file and rename it. For example, if your first draft is called Essay.doc, name the revised copy Essay2.doc. Revise the second copy. You can always open the old file to go back to your original version.

Proofreading Checklist

This checklist may help you as you proofread your work.

Sentences and Paragraphs

☑ Does every sentence have a subject and a predicate?

☑ Have you used the correct form for compound and complex sentences?

☑ Have you indented each paragraph?

Grammar and Usage

☑ Do your verbs agree with their subjects?

☑ Have you used subject and object pronouns correctly?

☑ Have you used the correct form of adjectives and adverbs that compare?

Capitalization and Punctuation

☑ Have you capitalized proper nouns and the pronoun *I*?

☑ Have you used commas correctly in compound sentences, addresses, dates, and series of words?

☑ Have you used apostrophes correctly?

☑ Have you surrounded all direct quotations with quotation marks?

Spelling

☑ Are you sure of the spelling of every word?

 Technology

Remember that a computer spell checker won't catch homophone mistakes. The computer will think this sentence is correct: *Their is know weigh out.* The sentence actually should be *There is no way out.* Because the mistakes are in meaning rather than spelling, the computer won't help you find them.

Presenting Your Work

For some kinds of writing, you are communicating to yourself. When you write a diary or class notes, you are the audience. Most writing, however, is meant to reach an audience. The final writing stage is to **publish** your work, or present it to your readers.

Choose a way to publish your work that makes sense. Here are some ideas that can help you connect your writing with your audience.

Strategies Good Writers Use

- Consider your audience when making design decisions. Will illustrations or photographs help your readers understand your ideas?

- Try publishing one piece of work in two ways to see which method you think is more effective.

Publishing Ideas for Any Type of Writing

- Read it aloud.

- Place it in a class reading library or post it on a bulletin board.

- Have a partner read it silently.

- Send it to a friend as an e-mail attachment.

Publishing Ideas for Descriptive Writing

- Use music to enhance your writing. Record yourself reading to music.

- Take or find photographs to create an illustrated essay or poem.

- Use art materials to make a pictorial brochure.

- Make your writing the centerpiece of a collage, poster, or other artwork.

Publishing Ideas for Narrative Writing

- Create an illustrated book for the classroom library.

- Direct a play or video based on your story.

- Share your story with students in another region by sending it as an e-mail attachment.

- Submit your writing to your school literary magazine.

- Enter your story in a writing contest.

- Include your story in a classroom anthology.

Publishing Ideas for Persuasive Writing

- Send your work as a letter to the editor of your school or local paper.

- Hold a classroom debate on the topic.

- Create a newsletter or pamphlet to distribute in your school or community.

- Give a speech to your class or to a school assembly.

- Post your work on your school's website.

 ## Technology

If you are using a computer, print out one page of your final draft to review your font and spacing choices. Make sure that your fonts are easy to read. You might choose a bolder display font for the title.

Publishing Ideas for Expository Writing

- Collect class essays in an anthology with a broad topic, such as American history or biology.

- Make a poster for the school hallway.

- Use specialized software to create a multimedia report.

- Create a table display for the classroom or for a school fair.

- Take over as "teacher," and instruct your classmates.

Giving a Multimedia Presentation

STEP 1 Reread your report. Choose information to show through photographs, a map, a poster, or other visual aids.

STEP 2 Look in the library for audio or video recordings to accompany your report. Download from the Internet any images or sounds that you can use. Prepare any charts or graphs.

STEP 3 Organize the equipment you need, such as a VCR, an audio player, or a computer.

STEP 4 Plan and practice your presentation. Decide when to stop and what to show or play. Ask a classmate to assist you with equipment.

STEP 5 Present your report with confidence. Speak loudly and clearly, looking at your audience. Answer questions at the end.

Strategies Good Writers Use

- Write legibly, or choose legible fonts.
- Leave adequate margins.
- Indent paragraphs.
- Put your name on your work.

Strategies for Making an Oral Presentation	Applying the Strategies
Make note cards.	• Write each main idea with major details on a note card. Put your cards in order and number them.
Use visual aids.	• Identify ideas to illustrate. Create pictures, charts, diagrams, music, video, or PowerPoint™ slides to add visual interest.
Practice.	• Practice in front of a mirror, a friend, or a family member, or tape your rehearsal. • Practice looking at your audience as you speak. Listeners will be more alert if you connect with them.
Present confidently.	• Share your ideas with a firm and clear voice. Be prepared to answer questions from your audience.

Strategies for Listeners

- Identify the speaker's purpose, main idea, and point of view.
- Evaluate whether the speaker effectively supports the main idea.
- Determine if you agree with the speaker. What parts of the presentation do you like best? Which parts are less effective?

Uppercase and Lowercase
Cursive Alphabet

A B C D E F G H I
J K L M N O P Q R
S T U V W X Y Z

a b c d e f g h i
j k l m n o p q r
s t u v w x y z

A B C D E F G H I
J K L M N O P Q R
S T U V W X Y Z

a b c d e f g h i
j k l m n o p q r
s t u v w x y z

Using E-Mail

Sending electronic mail, or e-mail, is a convenient way to communicate. However, there are a few important things you should remember about using e-mail.

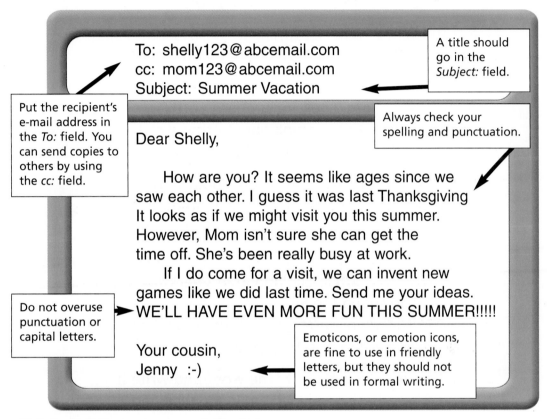

To: shelly123@abcemail.com
cc: mom123@abcemail.com
Subject: Summer Vacation

A title should go in the *Subject:* field.

Put the recipient's e-mail address in the *To:* field. You can send copies to others by using the *cc:* field.

Always check your spelling and punctuation.

Dear Shelly,

How are you? It seems like ages since we saw each other. I guess it was last Thanksgiving It looks as if we might visit you this summer. However, Mom isn't sure she can get the time off. She's been really busy at work.

If I do come for a visit, we can invent new games like we did last time. Send me your ideas. WE'LL HAVE EVEN MORE FUN THIS SUMMER!!!!!

Do not overuse punctuation or capital letters.

Your cousin,
Jenny :-)

Emoticons, or emotion icons, are fine to use in friendly letters, but they should not be used in formal writing.

E-Mail Manners and Safety

- Remember that you are writing a letter. Think about and use what you know about writing letters.

- Don't type in all capital letters. It looks as if you are shouting.

- Immediately tell an adult if you get a message that makes you uncomfortable.

- Never give your e-mail address or other personal information to strangers.

Spelling Strategies

Reading and writing will naturally improve your spelling, but you don't have to stop there. The following strategies can help you improve your spelling:

STEP 1 **Say the Word.** Speak slowly and listen for each syllable. Remember how you have heard the word used. Think about what it means.

STEP 2 **Analyze the Word.** Look for prefixes, suffixes, or other word parts you know. Think about other words that are related in meaning and spelling.

STEP 3 **Spell the Word to Yourself.** Think about how each sound can be spelled. For example, long o can be spelled o, oe, oa, ow, ough, and so on. Notice any unusual spelling.

STEP 4 **Write the Word While Looking at It.** Check the way you have arranged the letters. If you have not written the word clearly or correctly, write it again. Write difficult words two or three times.

STEP 5 **Check Your Learning.** Cover the word and write it again. Then check your spelling. If your spelling is incorrect, practice these steps again until the word becomes familiar to you.

Try This! Choose five of the commonly misspelled words below, and use the steps above to practice spelling them.

definitely	recommend	heroes
opinion	February	knowledge
eighth	separate	mysterious

Strategies for Making a Personal Spelling List	Applying the Strategies	Examples
Check your writing for words you have misspelled.	• Look for words with unusual spellings. • Circle each misspelled word.	• She is (illegible) for the swim team.
Find out how to spell the word correctly.	• Look up the word in a dictionary, glossary, or thesaurus.	• She is eligible for the swim team.
Write the word in your journal.	• Spell the word correctly. • Write a definition, synonym, or antonym of the word. • Use the word in a sentence.	• eligible— qualified, permitted to apply • He was not eligible because he was too young.
Use your spelling list to check your spelling as you write.	• Try to use new words often in your writing.	

Peer Conferences

In a **peer conference**, students come together to listen, respond, and share their writing. It's a meeting between writers. Everyone involved pays close attention to try to help one another communicate more effectively.

You will most likely hold a peer conference while you are revising. You will share the current draft of a work and discuss ways to improve it. This chart shows some strategies for getting the most out of a peer conference.

Strategies for Authors

Make copies of your work.

- If possible, make a copy of your draft for each person in the peer conference.

Read the work aloud.

- Read what you wrote. Don't add comments or excuses that aren't part of your writing.

- Ask another person to read your draft aloud. Hearing your work can help you recognize problems.

Listen and take notes.

- Listen to readings and comments on every work, not just your own. Use your notes to keep track of useful writing hints and your classmates' suggestions.

- Don't reject any ideas right away. Ask your classmates to explain any comments you do not understand.

Strategies for Reading Aloud

- Speak in a clear, loud voice.
- Read a little more slowly than you speak normally.
- Rehearse your reading at least once by yourself.

Strategies for Responders

Listen actively.

- Pay attention as the work is being read. Try to identify the main idea and the supporting details. Also listen for interesting language.

- Have a pen ready to jot down ideas that come to you while you're listening.

Make constructive comments.

- Identify specific words, sentences, and paragraphs that you like, and tell why. Then tell what doesn't work, and why.

- Be polite. Balance your criticism with praise for effective writing.

- Be accepting. When you make a suggestion, don't be hurt or angry if the writer does not agree. Remember that it's your classmate's writing, so he or she gets the final say.

Keep an open mind.

- Remember that everyone has a personal voice. Just because you might have written something differently doesn't mean it's wrong.

- Don't judge a piece of writing by whether you agree with the writer. The writer's opinion on an issue has nothing to do with the craft of writing.

Using Rubrics

Teachers often use checklists of criteria to evaluate writing. These guidelines are called **rubrics**. Rubrics list the key characteristics for grading writing, usually on a scale of 1 to 4 points or 1 to 6 points. The highest score reflects writing that is focused, relevant, and appropriate.

You can use rubrics to evaluate and improve your own work. Some writing assignments may give you a list of evaluation criteria. If not, create your own list of the key characteristics for the kind of writing that you are asked to do.

Here are some tips for using rubrics to help you during any stage of the writing process:

Before Writing

- Review the criteria on the checklist to remind yourself of the most important traits of the best writing.
- Use these criteria to help you plan your writing.

During Writing

- Check your draft against the rubric.
- Make notes about traits that you do not find in your draft, as well as those that can be improved.
- Use your evaluation to help you revise your draft.

After Writing

- Compare your finished writing against the list of criteria. Your final work should demonstrate all of the key characteristics expected of the best writing.
- If your writing still needs improvement, revise it again and make another copy.

Strategies Good Writers Use

- Proofreading can raise your score by at least a point. If you make several grammar and spelling mistakes, your teacher will give you a lower score.
- Make sure that your writing addresses the purpose and audience you have in mind.

Sometimes a rubric shows just the highest score. Here is a sample rubric for a research report. The highest score is 6 points.

SCORE OF 6 ★★★★★★

- ★ The research report fits the purpose for writing. The audience it was written for would understand it.
- ★ The report has a clear beginning that introduces the topic. The middle sections give logically organized information and ideas about the topic. The ending summarizes or draws a conclusion.
- ★ The report presents ideas and information from a variety of sources. The writer uses his or her own words.
- ★ The report has description, rich details, or narrative parts that add information about the topic. The ideas are interesting.
- ★ The report has transition words and phrases that help the reader understand how the ideas are related.
- ★ The sentences are written in a variety of ways to make the writing interesting to read.
- ★ The report has few errors in spelling, grammar, and punctuation.

What other characteristics do you think are important in a research report?

Writing for Tests

Many tests—especially standardized tests—include writing prompts, or topics for writing. These prompts are like any writing assignment, except that your work is usually timed. You can apply all of your writing craft to writing for tests.

Always begin by paying close attention to the prompt. It tells you what to write. You may need to interpret clue words in the prompt to identify your purpose, form, and audience.

Sample Writing Prompt

Think of a goal that you met in the last year. What steps did you take to meet your goal? Now write about your accomplishment. Include details about the steps you took and how you felt when you succeeded.

> This sentence introduces the topic.

> These directions suggest kinds of details you can use to develop the topic.

> This tells you your assignment. Since you are writing about your own experience, you can use the form of a personal narrative.

Types of Writing Found on Tests

Type of Writing	Purpose	Clue Words in the Prompt
Narrative	to entertain, to tell a story	tell a story, tell about a time, tell what happened
Informational	to explain or define	explain why, tell how, tell the cause of
Persuasive	to persuade or convince	persuade, tell why you think, explain why you would

Strategies for Interpreting a Prompt	Applying the Strategies
Read the prompt.	• Read to get a sense of the topic and form.
Identify the topic, purpose, and form of your assignment.	• Reread the prompt, looking for clue words that tell details about what you should write.
Restate your assignment.	• Silently summarize the assignment in your own words. For example, "I am supposed to write a letter that persuades my classmates to do community service."

Managing Your Time

On a writing test, you are given a set amount of time in which to prewrite, draft, and edit your work. If you plan ahead, you can finish your work within the time frame.

First, look at the time limit. Before you start work, set aside time for each writing stage. These pie charts show how you might divide your time.

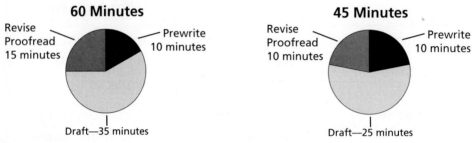

60 Minutes

Revise Proofread 15 minutes — Prewrite 10 minutes

Draft—35 minutes

45 Minutes

Revise Proofread 10 minutes — Prewrite 10 minutes

Draft—25 minutes

Strategies for Timed or Tested Writing	Applying the Strategies
Prewrite	• Write down your topic and form. • Brainstorm ideas. Use graphic organizers to help you organize your ideas.
Draft	• Use your prewriting notes to guide your draft. • Add details to develop your ideas as much as possible.
Revise/Proofread	• Clarify topic sentences. • Take out unrelated facts or details. • Check your punctuation, capitalization, grammar, and spelling.

Writing Models

Realistic Fiction

Realistic fiction tells a story that could be true but is not. It features characters and settings that are based on the real world.

Michael Jordan for a Day

Leon had always been short, even as a baby. This would not have been so bad, but Leon wanted to play basketball, and basketball players are tall. After all, the whole point of basketball is to toss a ball through a hoop several miles above the ground.

Leon tried out for the team anyway. He dribbled and passed well and even made a basket or two.

"Here's my Michael Jordan shot," said Leon. The ball whipped through the net.

Then the coach sent in Rick "The Stick" Walters to guard Leon. Rick Walters was named "The Stick" for a reason. He was thin and very, very tall. Poor Leon could not get past him and could not shoot over him.

> introduces the main character and the problem

> use of humor to add interest

> The writer uses sentences of different lengths for variety.

"Your Michael Jordan shot does you a lot of good now," sneered Stick.

"You're a good ball handler, Leon," said the coach. "I'll let you practice with the team, but I have to tell you the truth: Don't expect to play."

Leon practiced all season with the team. He worked hard. Even Stick was impressed.

During every game, Leon sat on the bench cheering. How he wanted to play! Toward the end of the season, one of the regular players was injured. Finally Leon got his chance. Stick was ready when the coach sent Leon in.

"I'll block Leon's guy and my own guy," said Stick. "Go, Leon." ← dialogue to move the action along

Leon did not have time to be surprised. He grabbed the ball and dribbled madly. No one could get to Leon because of Stick.

"Here's my Michael Jordan shot," he whispered. The ball whipped through the net. With Stick's help, Leon had won the game! ← ending that satisfies readers

Historical Fiction

Historical fiction is realistic fiction that takes place at a specific time in the past. Historical fiction relies on details of time and place to paint a picture of an earlier world.

Alicia Troy, Minutegirl

The year was 1775. All over Massachusetts, men were forming militias for the fight they feared would come. Benjamin Troy and his son Daniel joined the Minutemen in their town, Lexington. Every few days, they were called to drill. As the women of the town gathered in the square, they often saw the men marching up the main street.

Alicia Troy watched this with growing excitement. She was never content to sit home by the fire, darning her brother's socks or embroidering her sampler. She wished that she could drill with her father and brother.

One evening Alicia was left at home as the men went off to drill. As she sat glumly by the window spinning wool, she saw something frightening. A column of men in red coats was marching up the long road toward Lexington. If these British soldiers saw the Minutemen drilling, there might be trouble.

The beginning sets the scene.

cultural details from a specific time and place

The writer shares the character's emotions with the reader.

accurate historical details

Alicia ran out the back door and saddled her horse. She rode through the woods until she reached the clearing where the Minutemen drilled. She jumped off her horse and marched up to Colonel Adams.

"Colonel, there is a column of Redcoats perhaps ten minutes away," said Alicia.

The colonel disbanded his troops, and they scattered in all directions.

"Alicia Troy, you have done well," said the colonel. "You are a good spy and a clever girl. I will name you an honorary Minuteman."

"Thank you, Colonel," Alicia said, "but I would rather be called a Minutegirl!"

The colonel laughed, touched his hat, and rode off. Benjamin and Daniel hugged Alicia, and they rode home together.

Actions are described in time order.

dialogue to move the story forward

Folktale

Traditionally, a **folktale** is a story handed down from generation to generation. Folktales sometimes feature fantastic events and may teach a lesson. Some ancient folktales explain the origins of something in nature. Many modern folktales include the same elements.

Friends Forever

Long, long ago, meadows filled the lands between the mountains. The meadows were full of flowers of every color. Some of the most beautiful were striped with orange and black.

> time and place clearly indicated

In those days, the flowers could talk to one another and to all the passing breezes. Some of the breezes had traveled all the way to the sea. The orange-and-black flowers were spellbound by their stories of crashing waves and velvety fog.

> fantastic events

> problem introduced

"I wish I could see the ocean," one sighed. "It must be the most marvelous thing in the world."

"No, it isn't," said a small blue flower softly. "The most wonderful thing is to be right here in the meadow. I love to wake up in the spring and watch the year change."

Just then a magic breeze brushed by. "I've been listening to you," it said. "Do you really want to see the ocean?"

"Oh, yes," cried the orange-and-black flower.

"Then you shall have your wish," said the magic breeze.

The orange-and-black flower felt a gentle tug. Suddenly it was flying! It had been turned into a butterfly.

"Good-bye," called the blue flower.

"Good-bye," said the butterfly. "I'll be back to see you next year."

The butterfly kept its promise. Every year the orange-and-black monarch butterflies visit their old friends in the meadows and tell them stories of the sea. The other flowers, however, are content to stay in the meadows and watch the seasons come and go.

Lesson: Friends can like different things.

dialogue to move action along

problem solved

The ending explains a natural occurrence and teaches a lesson.

Myth

Myths usually explain natural events. They may include gods and goddesses, and they often involve supernatural acts.

The Pine Cone

At one time, the seeds of the pine tree were quite exposed. They were bright and shiny, and they were extremely attractive to birds and squirrels.

Alas, this meant that the seeds were eaten instead of dropping to the ground to develop into new pine trees. All over the land, pine trees were becoming scarce.

problem

At last, the chief goddess announced a contest. She would give a prize to the god or goddess who devised the best plan to protect the pine tree's seeds.

Time-order words help to sequence events.

Soon the gods met to share their ideas. The chief goddess called each one forward.

The god of secrets had designed a shining silver case for the pine seeds.

"I'm afraid this won't work. It will just make the seeds even more attractive to magpies and squirrels," said the chief goddess.

The goddess of the hunt had made a coating of prickly golden arrows for the pine seeds.

"This is good," said the chief goddess, "but it is too colorful. We may use this design for a meadow plant instead of for a tree."

dialogue to move the story forward

The god of war had made armor for the pine seeds, using a material that looked like wood.

supernatural explanation for natural occurrence

"Here is the winner," said the chief goddess. "This design not only protects the seeds but camouflages them as well."

Since that time, pine tree seeds have been enclosed in a woody armor. Pine trees are again found all over the land.

Tall Tale

A **tall tale** uses exaggeration and humor to tell a story. Its characters and their problems are larger than life.

The Floods of '25

Did you ever hear what caused the great floods of '25? Well, way up the river, right about where it starts, twin boys lived with their mom. One twin was as large as the other, and each was as large as a Douglas fir. In the spring of '25, Mom needed water for her garden, so one twin started digging a well. Pretty soon, he'd dug to the center of the earth. He had worked up a little sweat digging, so the other twin jumped in and took over.

It didn't take long for the twins to work their way through the earth to the other side. They came up in a huge lake. The twins went back home and drew water through straws. Pretty soon, Mom's garden had washed clear away, along with most of the Atchoo Valley. Now you know: It was Mom's well that caused the floods of '25.

informal, chatty tone

vivid language to spark interest

Exaggeration adds humor to the story.

silly explanation for real-life event

Rhymed Poem

Poetry can express a mood or paint a picture with just a few words. Poetry is usually written in rhythmic lines rather than in sentences. In a rhymed poem, syllable sounds are repeated at the ends of paired lines. For example, the following poem follows a *rhyme scheme*, or *pattern*, of a/b/a/b: the first and third lines rhyme, and the second and fourth lines rhyme.

A sleeping fawn,

A single crow—

Above, the dawn.

Still night below.

> a pattern of rhythm and rhyme

Unrhymed Poem

In **unrhymed poetry**, rhythm, figurative language, and imagery express a mood.

The quiet night

Gentle breathing of branches.

The sun creeps

Glinting edges of hilltops.

A crow calls

Shrill salute to the morning.

> imagery strengthened by rhythm

Play

A **play** tells a story through dialogue. Plays are meant to be acted out. Stage directions in parentheses indicate action and emotions, and dialogue moves the play forward.

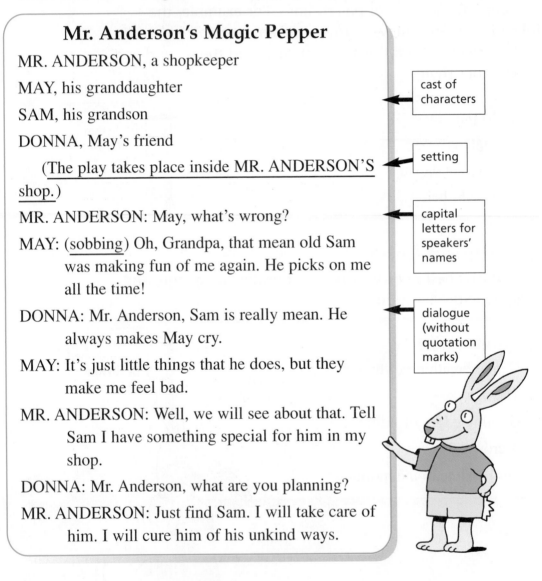

Mr. Anderson's Magic Pepper

MR. ANDERSON, a shopkeeper

MAY, his granddaughter

SAM, his grandson

DONNA, May's friend

> cast of characters

   (The play takes place inside MR. ANDERSON'S shop.)

> setting

MR. ANDERSON: May, what's wrong?

> capital letters for speakers' names

MAY: (sobbing) Oh, Grandpa, that mean old Sam was making fun of me again. He picks on me all the time!

DONNA: Mr. Anderson, Sam is really mean. He always makes May cry.

> dialogue (without quotation marks)

MAY: It's just little things that he does, but they make me feel bad.

MR. ANDERSON: Well, we will see about that. Tell Sam I have something special for him in my shop.

DONNA: Mr. Anderson, what are you planning?

MR. ANDERSON: Just find Sam. I will take care of him. I will cure him of his unkind ways.

(The girls exit. MR. ANDERSON picks up a pepper plant.)

stage directions to show action

(MAY and DONNA enter, followed by SAM.)

SAM: What have you got for me, Grandpa?

MR. ANDERSON: (calmly) This, Sam. It's a special pepper that will cure you.

stage directions to show emotions

SAM: Cure me? I'm not sick! Let's see it!

(MR. ANDERSON picks a small pepper and hands it to SAM.)

SAM: Big deal! A pepper. Who cares?

story moves along through dialogue

MR. ANDERSON: Not just a pepper—a very small pepper. It is just right for a big guy like you. Taste it!

(SAM bites the pepper, and tears begin to pour down his cheeks.)

SAM: It's hot! Waaaaaaah!

MAY: (astonished) Sam's crying!

MR. ANDERSON: Now he knows what it feels like when little things make you cry. Perhaps this ordinary little pepper will cure you, Sam, of causing tears in others.

satisfying conclusion

Descriptive Paragraph

A **descriptive paragraph** appeals to the reader's senses of sight, hearing, smell, touch, and taste. In a few words, it paints a picture of a subject. The reader should be able to visualize in his or her mind the scene or object being described.

Big Lake is prettiest just before sunset. The waves lap gently on the shoreline, and loons call eerily across the water. A breeze carries the spicy scent of pine trees. As the moon peeks above the horizon, the sky fades at the edges, first turning light blue, then lilac, then pink, and finally orange. The water is a mirror as streaky clouds are reflected on the lake. Bass and pickerel dance just below the shimmering surface, sometimes rising up to capture a mosquito. Everything is calm, and the water rests as still as glass.

topic sentence

vivid verbs

sensory details

Character Sketch

In a **character sketch**, a single person is described. The writer might tell how the character looks, sounds, and acts. The writer may explain or give opinions about the character by showing other people's reactions. The object is to create an engaging portrait in a few words.

Carla Washington rarely stood still as a child. She was always on the move in school. Today, Ms. Washington is the busy, successful, inspiring leader everyone predicted she would be. She is also the principal of our school.

> topic sentence

Ms. Washington strides into the school with a smile for everyone in her path. She knows every one of her students by name, and she makes each one feel special. No matter how busy she is, she always takes time to listen. No wonder her students voted her Educator of the Year.

> character reflected through eyes of others

When the last bell rings, most of us show signs of a long and hectic day. Ms. Washington, however, looks as fresh as when the day began. Her curly black hair is perfectly combed, her jacket is as straight as her spine, and she is still smiling. How does she do it?

> Comparisons make vivid word pictures.

Descriptive Essay

A **descriptive essay** is longer and more complete than a descriptive paragraph. Like a descriptive paragraph, however, it uses sensory details to paint a picture.

Morning in Barbados

When I am visiting my grandmother and aunt in Barbados, I find that I get up very early. I want to spend every possible moment outdoors. That is because mornings in Barbados are not like mornings anywhere else.

Morning in Barbados begins with the crow of a dozen roosters. Moments later, the clop-clop of hooves tells me that our neighbor is leaving for work. Wagon wheels whir and crunch over the rocky dirt road outside.

I run to the doorway and look out. To the east, the sun is a ball of fire over the ocean. The waves glisten as though they were brand new today. Seagulls wheel on the air currents over the cliffs.

introduction

sensory details in time order

figurative language

vivid verbs

Above my grandmother's house, a tree drips dew onto the tin roof. Fat chickens scurry through the yard, pecking at the grass and clucking at each other. I hear Grandmother stir and sigh.

To the west, the road disappears in a sugarcane field. The tall cane shines as the sun hits it. Soon the cane cutters will be working in the field, but now it stands silently, waiting. I stand silently, too, eagerly waiting for another Barbados day to begin.

Sequence words put sensory details in spatial order from east to west.

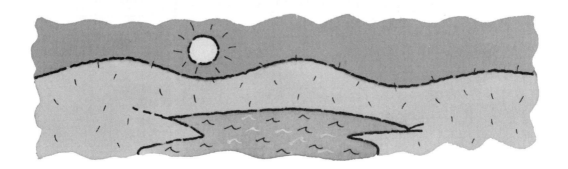

Personal Narrative

In a **personal narrative**, the writer tells about a personal experience. A personal narrative is autobiographical, but it typically focuses on a specific event.

Playing for Fun

I have always been miserable at sports. I cannot see balls when they fly at my head, and I always end up injuring myself or someone else. Once, I even managed all by myself to cause my softball team to lose the championship game in the ninth inning. It was not until our class picnic that I learned that even I can succeed at sports.

I was not even going to play in the volleyball game. After all, who would want me to play? The teams were uneven, however, and my friend Paul yelled at me to join. I was sure that everyone on the field was groaning inside, but they acted friendly as I stood stupidly in the back row.

A few volleys later, I realized something strange. No one was keeping score! I asked what the score was, and someone said, "Who knows? We're just playing for fun."

interesting opening

mix of sentence types

details in time order

We're just playing for fun? What a strange concept that was! If there were no score, then my clumsy efforts would not count. Suddenly I felt free to run for the ball. I even managed to hit it over the net — several times!

After the game, we all lay on the grass, exhausted. To the beat of my pounding heart, I kept thinking, "I wasn't bad. I wasn't bad." If you are any kind of athlete, you cannot imagine how difficult this was for me to accept. After all, I had been the worst athlete at whatever game I played for as long as I could remember.

direct appeal to audience

I am beginning to think that some people are just not meant to compete. These days, when I am in a competitive situation, I just pretend there is no score, grade, or judgment involved. When I simply "play for fun," everything comes easily to me.

ending that both summarizes and expands

Information Paragraph

An **information paragraph** gives condensed information about a specific topic.

> The United States contains several of the largest lakes in the world. Three of the Great Lakes are among the world's top ten lakes in square mileage. Lake Superior is the largest lake in this country, with an area of 31,700 square miles. Lakes Huron and Michigan have areas of 23,000 and 22,300 square miles, respectively. If you put all five Great Lakes together with their connecting waterways, they would form the largest body of fresh water anywhere in the world.

topic sentence

Details relate directly to the topic sentence.

Information Article

An **information article** gives details on a specific topic. It generally contains three or more paragraphs.

The Spingarn Medal

The Spingarn Medal is awarded each year by the NAACP for the highest achievement by an African American. It has been awarded to famous people and to little-known people who have made a difference.

introduction

Entertainers and athletes who have won the award include singer Lena Horne and baseball great Hank Aaron. In 1956 the medal went to Dr. Martin Luther King, Jr. The very next year, it was awarded to a group — Daisy Bates and the Little Rock Nine. Ms. Bates was president of the NAACP in Arkansas. In 1957 she and nine high school students were responsible for integrating a high school in Little Rock, Arkansas.

details and examples

Reading the list of winners of the Spingarn Medal is like reading a history of African Americans in the twentieth century. From Leontyne Price to Ralph Bunche, these are people who have made a difference. This award honors their outstanding contributions.

conclusion

Problem/Solution Paragraph

A **problem/solution paragraph** is organized around a given problem and the steps that lead to its solution. Usually, the problem is introduced in a topic sentence. The sentences that follow give steps in time order, and the paragraph ends with a concluding sentence that explains the solution and its significance.

Helping Hands Build a Stand

Our middle school sports complex was nearly completed, but there was no money left to build a concession stand. The Board of Education asked for community help. First, a local farmer donated the blocks to build the stand. Then an electrician and his son offered to do the wiring. Our principal sent out notices telling everyone to meet on Saturday for the stand-raising. Nearly 60 workers turned out to build the stand. It took all day, but by Saturday night, the final piece of our sports complex was done.

The title relates to the main idea.

topic sentence

transition words to make sequence clear

conclusion describes solution

How-to Essay

A **how-to essay** is a piece of informational writing that explains how to perform an action or complete a process. The essay names any materials that are needed. Steps are given in order, so that a careful reader could duplicate the action or process being described.

How to Make a Gas

You can make a gas out of a solid and a liquid. You will need a bottle, a funnel, a balloon, vinegar, and bicarbonate of soda. An old soda bottle will work just fine, but rinse it first.

Begin by pouring about two inches of vinegar into the bottle. Then use the funnel to pour some soda into the balloon. Next, fit the balloon over the neck of the bottle. Once it is tightly fitted, shake the balloon so that the soda drops into the bottle.

If you have followed the steps, you should see the soda and vinegar fizz up, and the balloon begin to expand. The mixture of soda and vinegar will give off the gas called carbon dioxide.

The title names the action or process.

All necessary materials are listed up front.

Transition words and phrases make the order of steps clear.

The conclusion sums up the action or process.

Essay of Explanation

An **essay of explanation** tells how or why something happens. A five-paragraph essay includes an introduction that presents the main idea, three paragraphs that provide reasons or examples that support the main idea, and a conclusion that wraps up the essay in an interesting way.

What It Takes to Live in the Desert

It's not easy to survive in the harsh environment of a desert. The bright sun burns all day, scorching the land and causing the temperature to soar far above 100 degrees. Then, when nighttime comes, temperatures can tumble below freezing. Because the air is warm and clouds seldom form, deserts have very little rain. Yet, despite these difficult conditions, the desert does have plant and animal life.

Plants that survive in the desert must compete for the limited supply of water, so they grow far apart. Some plants, such as the mesquite tree, have very deep roots that can locate water far below the surface of the earth. Other plants, including the barrel cactus, store water in their large trunks.

vivid words

Organization focuses first on plants, then on animals.

Animals that live in the desert have made many unusual adaptations to survive the difficult conditions. Most desert animals look for food at night to avoid the intense daylight heat. Small animals, such as snakes and rodents, dig burrows underground and stay there all day to keep cool.

change in topic starts new paragraph

Large animals try to stay in the shade during the day. These animals get their water from food and from the few water holes scattered across the desert. Some desert animals, like the famous camel, can convert stored fat into water. The fat is stored in the humps on the camel's back.

example

Obviously, deserts cannot support the huge variety of plants and animals that live in more humid climates. However, the number of plants and animals that have been able to adapt to desert conditions is much larger than one would have thought.

The conclusion wraps up the essay and refers back to the main idea.

Summary

A **summary** is a condensed version of written material. It includes:
• the main idea or ideas.
• the most important facts that support the main idea.

When you write a summary, you use your own words. Summarizing information helps you understand and remember it better.

Underground caves are usually found in areas made of limestone, a type of soft rock. Caves are formed when water wears away, or erodes, the surrounding rock. This erosion takes place over thousands of years.

> source article to be summarized

The shape of a cave depends on how soft the layers of limestone are. Sometimes erosion carves narrow, deep caves called sinkholes. Water flowing through such a cave would look like an underground waterfall! At other times, erosion makes caves whose floors are horizontal, or mostly on one level.

Water can also create different shapes inside a cave. Limestone contains a mineral called calcite. When water seeps down from the outside, through the cave's roof, the calcite dissolves. As water evaporates, the calcite is left behind. Drop by drop the calcite builds on top of itself. Over thousands of years, it forms cone-shaped stalactites that hang from the ceiling. Sometimes the water drips onto the cave's floor. The cone-shaped forms that grow up from the floor are called stalagmites.

Summary I

Water erosion creates underground caves. They are usually in places made of limestone because it is a soft rock. Erosion of the limestone sometimes makes caves that go up and down. At other times it makes horizontal caves. The different shapes inside a cave are created by the calcite in the water. Dripping water gradually makes cone shapes. Stalactites hang down and stalagmites stick up.

Summary II

Water erosion of limestone creates underground caves and the cone shapes inside them.

This summary states the main idea, summarizes how caves are formed, and briefly explains why certain shapes are found in them.

This is a one-sentence summary of the main idea of the passage.

Classification Essay

A **classification essay** shows how a large category of things—for example, books, vehicles, or animals—can be broken down into smaller groups that share a particular characteristic.

The Four Worlds of Reptiles

Reptiles come in a variety of colors, shapes, and sizes. However, they all share certain characteristics. All reptiles have dry, scaly skin, and they all breathe by means of lungs. Reptiles are cold-blooded, which means that their body temperature changes with the temperature of their surroundings. Because all reptiles have backbones, they are all part of the class of animals called vertebrates.

Zoologists divide reptiles into four major groups. The first group consists of lizards and snakes. This is the largest reptile group, with nearly 6,000 species existing today. They live mostly in deserts and other warm places.

> topic sentence

> variety of sentences

The second group consists of turtles. These are the only reptiles with a shell. There are about 200 species of turtles living in warm or hot climates in most parts of the world.

The paragraphs are organized by subtopics, each dealing with a different group of reptiles.

The third group is the crocodilians, which includes alligators and crocodiles. There are only 23 species of crocodilians. Most live in the fresh waters and lowlands of the tropics.

examples

The smallest group, with only 2 species, is the tuatara. The tuatara looks like a lizard but is more closely related to the dinosaurs. It lives on several islands off the coast of New Zealand.

Even though lizards, snakes, turtles, alligators, crocodiles, and tuataras are very different, they share certain characteristics that make them all members of the reptile family.

conclusion

Paragraph That Contrasts

A **paragraph that contrasts** shows how two things are different. To write an effective contrast paragraph, start with two things that have something in common. You might contrast a cat and a lion, for example, or how a bird and a plane fly. The common features make the differences stand out and make the contrast interesting.

Bald eagles and ospreys have a lot in common, and they are often mistaken for each other. However, there are several important differences that can help you to tell these two birds apart. Seen from below, the bald eagle is mostly dark, whereas the osprey is mostly light. The bald eagle soars with flat wings, but the osprey has a crook in its wings. Bald eagles eat fish that are dead or on the verge of dying. Ospreys, on the other hand, are the only large birds of prey that dive feet first into the water to capture live fish.

The writer uses a variety of sentences for interest.

vivid words

Transition words, such as *while, but,* and *on the other hand,* point out differences.

Comparison and Contrast Essay

A **comparison** shows how two subjects are alike. A **contrast** shows how they differ. Sometimes comparison and contrast are used in a single piece of writing.

Because they have a lot in common, bald eagles and ospreys are often mistaken for each other. Both are extremely large birds of prey. They often live in the same territory, and you may see either type of bird soaring gracefully above the earth. Both hunt mostly fish.

> topic sentence

> points of comparison

If you know what to look for, however, you can tell these birds apart. Seen from below, the bald eagle is mostly dark, but the osprey is mostly light. The bald eagle soars with flat wings, but the osprey has a crook in its wings. Bald eagles prefer to eat fish that are dead or that are on the verge of dying. Ospreys, on the other hand, are the only large birds of prey that dive feet first into the water to capture live fish.

> topic sentence

> points of contrast

Response to Literature

A **response to literature** presents a writer's personal thoughts about a work of literature. The writer expresses an opinion about some part of the work—for example, a character, the setting, events from the plot, or the theme of the story. The writer also includes details from the book to support his or her opinion.

The House of Dies Drear
by Virginia Hamilton

Imagine that you are about to enter an old house built more than 150 years ago. You know that the building is rumored to be haunted and to hold a buried treasure. You discover secret tunnels and passageways once you are inside. You find strange objects that may be clues to the secrets of the old house. Now imagine that you and your family are about to move into this unusual home.

Would you be curious to know more? Would you be frightened to live in such a place? This is the situation that thirteen-year-old Thomas faces at the beginning of The House of Dies Drear by Virginia Hamilton.

The introduction grabs the reader's interest and introduces the house as the main focus of this response.

the title and author

Thomas's father is a college professor, and he bought the house because his main interest is the Underground Railroad. It turns out that the house was once owned by a man named Dies Drear. The house was a main stopping point, or station, on the Underground Railroad during the Civil War.

important details about background and setting

As Thomas explores the house, he learns about the real Underground Railroad, a series of homes and businesses owned by people who helped African Americans escape from slavery in the South to freedom in the North. Thomas learns about the dangerous journey that these brave slaves took with the help of abolitionists, Northerners who wanted to end slavery.

The writer tells how Thomas responds to the setting and shares more important facts about the history of the house.

The more I learned about the history of the house and what it stood for, the more I felt as if it were a living, breathing character. As the secrets of the house were revealed, I began to understand what life was like during the Civil War and how important the issue of slavery was to our country. When my heart stopped pounding, I went to my computer to learn more about the Underground Railroad, and I haven't stopped yet!

The writer describes how the old house comes alive as a character and how the book influenced him or her.

Persuasive Essay

In a **persuasive essay**, the writer tries to convince an audience of his or her opinion on a particular topic. A good persuasive essay uses logic to support its argument.

Soccer Is Here to Stay

It should be clear to everyone at Baker Middle School that we should add soccer to our list of school sports. Soccer is not just a passing fad. It is here to stay.

→ thesis statement

At one time, soccer was unpopular in our country. Today, however, you can see it more and more often on television. It has always been popular in Europe, South America, and Asia. Many students at our school have cultural backgrounds from these parts of the world. Quite a few of them have expressed a desire to play soccer, but our school has no team for them to join.

→ logical support for opinion

Soccer is a game that involves fancy footwork, steady nerves, and stamina. It is fun to play and fun to watch. If we start a soccer team at Baker, nearly half of the school will turn out to cheer the team on. Baker knows that soccer is here to stay.

Persuasive Letter

The purpose of a **persuasive letter** is to express an opinion and to convince someone else of the validity of your opinion. A persuasive letter can be to a person, a group, a business, or a publication. A letter to the editor of a local newspaper is a common example of persuasive writing.

14 Clover Lane
Freeville, NY 13068
March 3, 200-

Editor
Freeville Express
386 Main Street
Freeville, NY 13068

Dear Editor:

    Your recent articles on the fires at Hayes Department Store and Memorial Hospital lead to one conclusion: Freeville needs its own volunteer fire department. ← **thesis statement**

The firefighters from Middletown and Upper Meadow deserve our praise and gratitude. ← **supporting details**

However, our town is now large enough to bear the responsibility for its own safety. Furthermore, fire-fighting services could be delivered more efficiently if personnel and equipment did not have to travel the extra miles from these other towns. What can be more important than providing for the safety of our families?

            Sincerely,

            Howard Sutfin

Book Review

A **book review** gives an opinion about a book the writer has read. It supports that opinion with details from the book.

Journey to the Center of the Earth by Jules Verne is the exciting story of three daring explorers. They travel to Iceland and enter an extinct volcano. Once inside, they travel down toward the center of the earth. Along the way, they find prehistoric plants and an underground ocean, complete with hideous monsters. The explorers make wonderful discoveries, but will they ever be able to return home?

Although this book was published more than one hundred years ago, it is still thrilling. If you like science fiction, you will enjoy Journey to the Center of the Earth.

title

author

summary

opinion

Movie Review

A **movie review** expresses the writer's opinion about a movie and supports that opinion with details from the movie.

I do not understand why so many people like the movie Day of the Dinosaurs. Although the special effects are amazing, I think it is too skimpy on plot, too different from the book, and much too violent. ← title ← opinion

There is very little plot at all. The movie is one big car chase, except that some of the "cars" are dinosaurs. The book is much better at telling you what is happening and why. The movie concentrates on scaring its viewers. I think younger kids might have nightmares if they were allowed to see it on video. ← reasons

If you like suspense—and dinosaurs—my advice is to read the book. If you love special effects, rent the movie and fast-forward past the boring parts.

News Story

A **news story** contains a *headline*, a *lead*, and a *body*. It gives information about a current event, an issue, or a person.

Sanchez Seeks Presidency of School Board

headline

Maria Sanchez, a local business executive, is running for president of the school board in Duane County this year because she wants to make the board more responsive to the needs of students and their taxpaying parents.

lead telling *who, what, where, when,* and *why*

Sanchez, who grew up in Duane County and attended its public schools, says she wants to help students realize their full potential. She wants the board to focus on keeping potential dropouts in school and on spending tax dollars where they can do the most good.

body telling *how*

"Head Start and Students in Business are examples of two successful programs I would continue to support," Sanchez says. "Let's fund programs that work."

Sanchez would like to change the way board meetings are run. If elected, she would encourage students to participate as nonvoting members of the board. Sanchez believes she can accomplish most of these changes within the first six months if she is elected.

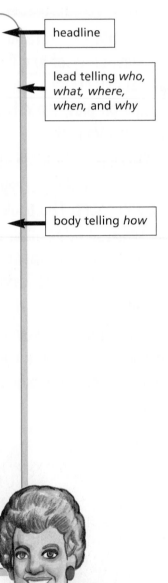

Friendly Letter

One of the most common forms of everyday writing is the **friendly letter**. A writer may send letters for any purpose: to entertain, to describe, to inform, or to persuade.

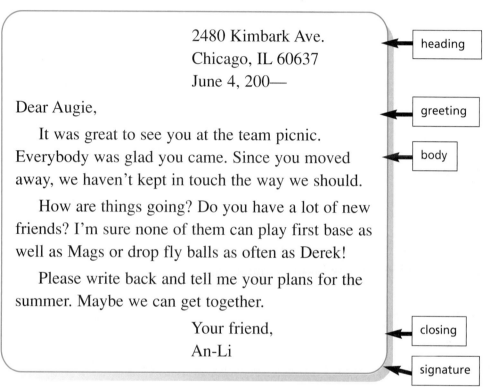

2480 Kimbark Ave.
Chicago, IL 60637
June 4, 200—

← heading

Dear Augie,

← greeting

    It was great to see you at the team picnic. Everybody was glad you came. Since you moved away, we haven't kept in touch the way we should.

← body

    How are things going? Do you have a lot of new friends? I'm sure none of them can play first base as well as Mags or drop fly balls as often as Derek!

    Please write back and tell me your plans for the summer. Maybe we can get together.

                   Your friend,

← closing

                   An-Li

← signature

Business Letter

A **business letter** is more formal than a friendly letter. It may be sent to inform, to persuade, or to request information.

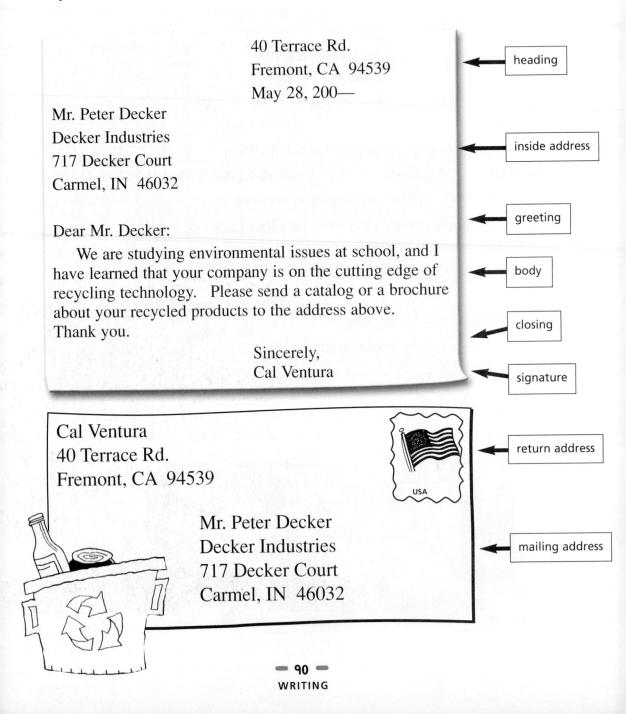

40 Terrace Rd.
Fremont, CA 94539
May 28, 200—

← heading

Mr. Peter Decker
Decker Industries
717 Decker Court
Carmel, IN 46032

← inside address

Dear Mr. Decker:

← greeting

We are studying environmental issues at school, and I have learned that your company is on the cutting edge of recycling technology.   Please send a catalog or a brochure about your recycled products to the address above. Thank you.

← body

Sincerely,
Cal Ventura

← closing

← signature

Cal Ventura
40 Terrace Rd.
Fremont, CA 94539

← return address

USA

Mr. Peter Decker
Decker Industries
717 Decker Court
Carmel, IN 46032

← mailing address

Forms

People complete **forms** to join clubs and organizations, apply for jobs, order merchandise, return merchandise, and so on. Every form is different, so the only rules are these: Follow the directions, and write neatly!

MEMBERSHIP APPLICATION (Please print)
Seattle Boys Club

Name ___**Rolle**_____**Carl**_____**M.**___ ← neat handwriting
         (last)   (first)   (m.i.)

Address ____**2225 First Avenue**_____
             (Street)

____**Seattle**_____**WA**_____**98121**_____
   (City)   (State)   (Zip)

Age __**13**___ School **Evergreen Middle School**_____

Height _**5' 4"**___ Weight _____**128**_____

Activities

(Please pick 3 and number in order of interest.)

____	baseball	____	gymnastics	____	soccer
_**1**_	basketball	____	karate	____	swimming
_**2**_	choir	_**3**_	photography	____	tai chi

Please suggest other activities you would like to see offered.

__**volleyball, woodworking**_____

_____

Research Report: Note Taking

Note taking is expressing in your own words the key ideas and important details that you have read or heard, usually in a shortened form. You can take notes to study for tests or to prepare spoken or written presentations. These hints can help you when you are taking notes:

- Include important words or phrases.
- Define new terms.
- Use abbreviations that make sense to you.
- Include the source of the information so that you can go back to it if necessary.

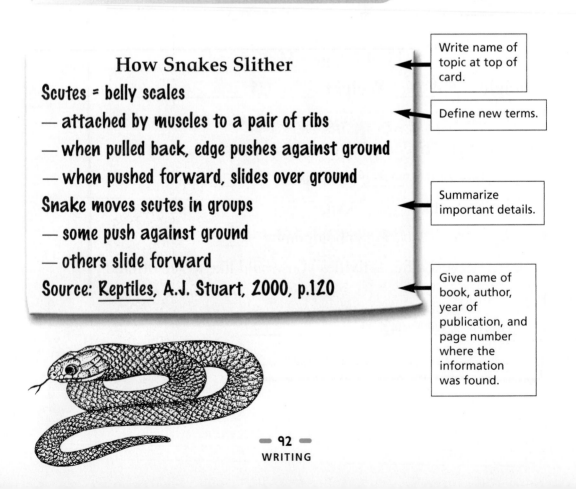

How Snakes Slither

Scutes = belly scales
— attached by muscles to a pair of ribs
— when pulled back, edge pushes against ground
— when pushed forward, slides over ground
Snake moves scutes in groups
— some push against ground
— others slide forward
Source: <u>Reptiles</u>, A.J. Stuart, 2000, p.120

Write name of topic at top of card.

Define new terms.

Summarize important details.

Give name of book, author, year of publication, and page number where the information was found.

Research Report: Outline

Lengthy informative writing, such as a research report, may be organized by using an **outline**. An outline uses Roman numerals for main topics, capital letters for subtopics, and Arabic numerals for details.

How Snakes Slither

I. Introduction

II. Methods of Movement ← main topic

  A. Crawling or "Walking on Ribs" ← Never use an A without a B.

    1. Scutes or belly scales attached to ribs by muscles ← Never use a 1 without a 2.

    2. Pulling scales back pushes them against ground

    3. Pushing scales forward slides them over ground

  B. Waves

    1. Flexing muscles produces waves

    2. Curves of body push against ground to move snake forward

  C. Sidewinding

    1. Snake arches body upward and throws head to one side

    2. Snake pulls body across and throws head to other side

III. Conclusion

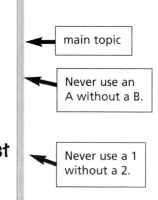

Research Report—Science

A **science report** relies on facts and information from several sources. The writer usually attempts to answer a question.

How Snakes Slither

Long ago, people believed that snakes walked on their ribs. They thought that the ribs acted as if they were several pairs of legs. We know now that this is not true. How then do snakes slither? ← *a topic that is not too broad*

Along a snake's belly lie rows of overlapping scutes, or scales. Each scute is attached by muscles to a pair of the snake's ribs. When a scute is pulled back by the muscles, its edge pushes against the ground. When the scute is pushed forward by the muscles, it slides over the ground. ← *specialized words defined and explained*

A snake moves the overlapping scutes on its belly in groups. With each movement, some scutes push against the ground, and others slide forward. This allows the snake to move forward in a straight line.

In another common method of movement, the snake flexes its muscles to produce a series of waves down the length of its body. The curves of the body push against the ground, moving the snake forward.

A few desert snakes use a strange form of movement called sidewinding. The snake arches the front of its body upward and throws its head to one side. It then pulls its body across and throws its head to the other side. Because sand gives the snake little to push against, sidewinding works better than do other forms of movement.

supporting details

Describing in detail the way snakes move makes their movements sound jerky. In fact, their movements are very smooth and efficient. Undulating muscles and overlapping scutes move snakes forward steadily at an average speed of about two miles per hour.

Research Report—Social Studies

A **social studies report** may give information about a single topic, or it may compare and contrast more than one topic. As with any research report, the writer uses a variety of sources to gather information.

Voting Rights—The Road to Equality

title

Throughout most of American history, women did not enjoy the same rights as men. They could not own land. They could not make decisions about how their children were to be educated. Most importantly, they could not vote.

introduction

In the 1820s and 1830s, a number of white women began protesting the inequalities of slavery. It was through this struggle for human rights that they began to see the more subtle inequalities in their own lives.

details in time order

In 1848 a number of important women activists, including Elizabeth Cady Stanton and Lucretia Mott, organized a women's suffrage convention at Seneca Falls, New York.

The delegates to the convention issued a proclamation based on the Declaration of Independence. In the document, they said that "all men and women are created equal." They demanded that women be given "all the rights and privileges which belong to them as citizens of the United States."

— quotations from another source

Winning these rights took longer than expected. During the 1890s, several of the new western states gave women the right to vote. Eventually, some of the eastern and midwestern states did likewise. However, women still could not vote in national elections. That right was finally won in 1920 when the Nineteenth Amendment to the Constitution was ratified. At last, the right to have a say in the way the country is governed applied to its male and female citizens.

— details in time order

— summarizing statement

Creating Professional-Looking Documents

You know that writing is a form of communication. It begins with the writer and ends with the reader. As a writer, you should work to make the connection between you and your reader as clear as possible.

It does you no good to revise and proofread your way to a brilliant paper if smudges, awkward spacing, and illegible type make that paper impossible to read. You can follow these rules to make sure your documents are clean and professional looking:

Margins

- Margins for reports and other papers should be a minimum of one inch on both the left and the right.
- If you plan to put your paper in a binder or attach pages on the left-hand side, you may wish to make the left-hand margin one and one-half inches wide.
- Make the top margin on the first page two inches deep. On all other pages, the top and bottom margins may be one inch deep.

Spacing

- Double-space your work.
- Indent the first line of each paragraph five spaces.
- Don't end a page with the first line of a paragraph. If you can't fit two lines, start the paragraph on the next page.
- If your report includes footnotes, leave room for them at the bottom of the page.

Strategies Good Writers Use

- Think about your audience. What font should you use? Should you use large or small type?
- Consider whether illustrations or diagrams might make your ideas easier to understand.

Strategies for Using Visual Aids	Applying the Strategies
Present or repeat important material in chart form.	• Decide what your title and headings should be. Present the information in the most logical way.
Explain something that is hard to visualize by using an illustration or diagram.	• Think about what your reader needs to see in order to understand the concept.
Use a diagram to show the relationship between ideas.	• Venn diagrams can show comparisons and contrasts. Tree diagrams or flowcharts can show how things are connected.

 ## Technology

You can add graphics to your word-processed document in a number of ways. You can create graphics in a different program and paste them in place or into a table or frame, or you can use *Table* and *Borders* to create charts.

Creating a Footnote

Follow these steps to add **footnotes** to your text:

STEP 1 **Number the Text.** Type a superscript (^{1}) number after the word or sentence you wish to footnote. Number your footnotes consecutively throughout your report.

STEP 2 **Create the Footnote.** Use the following style:

---

[1]K. A. Zahler, *21st Century Office Assistant's Manual* (New York: Dell Publishing, 1995), p. 187.

STEP 3 **Insert the Footnote.** Type a horizontal underscore one or two inches long following the last line of text on your page. Then type your footnote at the bottom of the page or use *Insert* and then *Footnote* in your word processing program.

> **Strategies Good Writers Use**
>
> • Put your name on your work.
> • Use footnotes and a bibliography to give credit for quoted material.

Adding a Header or Footer

Headers are lines at the top of a page that add identifying information.

EXAMPLE: Marc Nolte, World History 1, The Bronze Age.......1

Footers are lines at the bottom of a page that add identifying information.

EXAMPLE: October 15, 2003   page 4

Either a header or a footer may include a page number. On a computer, add a header or footer by choosing *View* and then *Header and Footer* in your word processing program. Click *Close* to return to your document.

Creating a Bibliography

List all the sources you have used in a bibliography on a separate page.

 Create the Bibliographical Reference
Use the following style:

For a Book:
Zahler, K. A. *21st Century Office Assistant's Manual.* New York: Dell Publishing, 1995.

For a Chapter:
Katz, Audrey. "Business Reports," *Webster's New World Secretarial Handbook.* New York: Prentice-Hall, 1989.

For an Article:
Jones, Deirdre. "Better Report Writing." *English Journal*, Vol. VII (May 2001): 25–28.

For an Online Reference:
Hoffman, Daria. "Typewriter." *World Book Online Americas Edition*, http://www.aolsvc.worldbook.aol.com/wbol/wbPage/na/ar/co/572800, May 14, 2001.

 Arrange Your References
References should be arranged alphabetically by last name of author.

Et al. and _____,
- If a publication has more than three authors, list the publication under the name of the first mentioned author and then use *and others* or *et al.*
- If two or more works by the same author are cited, instead of typing the author's name over and over, use a solid line of five underscores followed by a comma in place of the name.

Creating a Title Page

Any report or story looks better with a clear **title page**.

STEP 1 **Center the Title.** If you are using a word processor, use *Center* to place your title evenly horizontally. If your title is long, break it logically. Center it vertically as well.

STEP 2 **Include Your Name.** A title page should include the author's name. Your school or class may have a particular style to use. Here is an example:

THE SECRET LIFE OF RED NEWTS
BY NORMAN LAFEBER

Creating a Table of Contents

After typing and numbering the pages of a long report or group project, you may choose to create a **table of contents**.

STEP 1 **Type CONTENTS in Capital Letters.** Center this heading two inches down from the top of the page.

STEP 2 **Type Each Chapter or Section Heading.** Major headings should be in capital letters. Subheadings may be capital and lowercase, indented under the major headings.

STEP 3 **Add Leaders and Page Numbers.** Leaders draw the reader's eye across to the correct page number.

CONTENTS

INTRODUCTION 2
PROBLEM 3
METHODS 5
   Field Test 7
   Survey 9
CONCLUSION 13

Grammar, Usage, and Mechanics

SENTENCES; INTERJECTIONS

- A **declarative sentence** makes a statement and ends with a period.

- An **interrogative sentence** asks a question and ends with a question mark.

- An **imperative sentence** gives a command or makes a request. Most imperative sentences end with a period.

- An **exclamatory sentence** expresses strong feeling and ends with an exclamation point.

- An **interjection** is a word or a group of words that expresses strong feeling.

Write whether each sentence is *declarative* or *interrogative*.

1. **Several teachers heard Boyd yelling.**
2. **What is he upset about?**
3. **Why does Imogene want margarine?**
4. **Imogene's idea was very clever.**
5. **Jolene had to take Boyd home.**

Write whether each sentence is *imperative* or *exclamatory*. Write any interjections.

6. **Hold still.**
7. **Wow! What a greasy mess!**
8. **What a nice compliment!**
9. **Speak louder.**
10. **Hurrah! We won!**

SENTENCES; INTERJECTIONS

The school paper is running a story about Boyd and the bike rack. Your job is to edit the sentences, adding capital letters and correct end marks. Then write whether each sentence is *declarative*, *interrogative*, *imperative*, or *exclamatory*.

1. did you hear about Boyd Liggett and the bike rack

2. well, let me tell you about it

3. Boyd got his head stuck in the bike rack

4. how did it happen

5. no one knows for certain

6. who rescued Boyd from this near disaster

7. the heroine was our very own Imogene

8. how clever she was

9.–10. The story writer had to leave to cover another story. Add two sentences to complete her story. Then identify the kinds of sentences you wrote.

CUMULATIVE REVIEW

Write *sentence* or *not a sentence* to tell whether each group of words is a sentence.

1. Gee whiz!
2. Why Boomer's face red?
3. Oh, he gets embarrassed very easily.
4. Give me an idea for a compliment.
5. The cup on the table.
6. Hand me that pen.

Write the sentences correctly, using capital letters and end marks. Then write whether each sentence is *declarative, imperative, interrogative,* or *exclamatory.* Circle each interjection.

7. what did they say about Imogene
8. Maxine couldn't spell two words
9. i thought Imogene was clever
10. where did the margarine come from
11. give me that list of compliments
12. wow what a brave thing to do
13. where did Boyd go
14. look he's over there

COMPLETE AND SIMPLE SUBJECTS

- The **subject** of a sentence names the person or thing the sentence is about.

- The **predicate** tells what the subject is or does.

- The **complete subject** includes all the words that name the person or thing the sentence is about.

- The **simple subject** is the main word or words in the complete subject. Sometimes the simple subject and the complete subject are the same.

Write each sentence, drawing one line under the complete subject and two lines under the predicate.

1. The woman in the poster wore a green satin gown.

2. Julian's mother had been a *chanteuse*.

3. That word means "a female singer" in French.

4. Stage performers interested Ethan.

5. The large poster seemed mysterious.

Write the complete subject of each sentence. Then write the simple subject. If the subject is *you* (understood), write *you*.

6. Mr. Singh wanted the pumpkins for something special.

7. The payment for the pumpkins was a ten-dollar bill.

8. The ten-dollar bill had a note.

9. The small note contained instructions.

10. Look in *Alice's Adventures in Wonderland.*

11. The book was on the shelf in the living room.

COMPLETE AND SIMPLE SUBJECTS

1.–8. Write the thank-you letter that Nathan wrote to his parents. Using a simple subject from the box, replace each number to write complete sentences.

food	**you**	**Cathy**	**scenery**
ocean	**water**	**I**	**sand**

Dear Mom and Dad,

Thank you so much for taking me camping! The **(1)** ____ was beautiful. The **(2)** ____ you cooked over the fire was delicious. **(3)** ____ also enjoyed swimming in the river. The **(4)** ____ was so warm! Next summer, **(5)** ____ should let me plan our trip. My friend **(6)** ____ suggested that we go to the beach. The **(7)** ____ and the **(8)** ____ are so much fun!

Love,

Nathan

9.–15. Write the complete subject of each of Nathan's sentences.

CUMULATIVE REVIEW

Write *sentence* or *not a sentence* to tell whether each group of words is a sentence.

1. Julian read the note carefully.
2. Written carefully on self-sticking notes.
3. Have you ever been to a party like that?
4. What a good time!
5. Couldn't find the book.

Write the sentences correctly, using capital letters and end marks. Then write whether the sentence is *declarative, interrogative, imperative,* or *exclamatory*. Circle each interjection.

6. i can't find that book
7. what is its title
8. look on the third shelf
9. hey what a memory you have
10. how did I miss it

Write each sentence. Underline the complete subject and circle the simple subject.

11. A clever puzzle might make a good gift.
12. The video store carried lots of puzzles.
13. One of the puzzles had a painting of water lilies.
14. The young boy wrapped his gift carefully.
15. His present would please Julian.

COMPLETE AND SIMPLE PREDICATES

- The **complete predicate** includes all the words that tell what the subject of the sentence is or does.
- The **simple predicate** is the main word or words in the complete predicate. Sometimes the simple predicate and the complete predicate are the same.

Write the complete predicate of each sentence.

1. We recited the pledge.
2. The official started the game.
3. Players must be gracious losers.
4. Good sportsmanship is important.
5. Our team lost no games at all.
6. We entered the state playoffs.
7. We played our games well.
8. The team celebrated its title victory.

Write the complete predicate of each sentence. Then write the simple predicate.

9. The boy read the list of batting averages.
10. The young shortstop memorized the numbers easily.
11. A baseball encyclopedia helped.
12. He found the book at the library.
13. The book was full of baseball history.
14. He wrote a report about baseball history.
15. His teacher liked his report.

COMPLETE AND SIMPLE PREDICATES

1.–8. A reporter wrote these sentences for a news article about Jerry's championship team. Write the complete predicate of each sentence. Then write the simple predicate.

(1) Jerry's team won every game in its league. **(2)** His team's average winning score was 12 to 1. **(3)** His team triumphed by 24 to 0 in one of the games. **(4)** His team achieved one victory in a strange way. **(5)** The other team's players forfeited the game. **(6)** Ben's team lost two out of three games to Jerry's team. **(7)** The Norristown boys swept all three games in the playoffs. **(8)** They beat Ellwood City in the final state championship game.

9.–10. Add two sentences of your own to the article. Underline the complete predicate and circle the simple predicate in each sentence.

CUMULATIVE REVIEW

Write the complete subject of each sentence. Then write the simple subject.

1. That player stole a base.
2. He may steal another.
3. Another hit would help us win.
4. Your older brother plays on another team.
5. His team has the best record.
6. Most spectators cheer loudly at games.

Write the sentences correctly, using capital letters and end punctuation. Write whether each sentence is *declarative, interrogative, imperative,* or *exclamatory.* Circle the interjections.

7. which team is your favorite
8. watch the Norristown team
9. wow what a great catch
10. both teams have good players

Write the complete predicate of each sentence. Then write the simple predicate.

11. The umpires held a conference.
12. The next batter swung wildly at the ball.
13. The lead runner is now at third base.
14. The pitcher pitched the next ball very carefully.
15. The player hit the ball well.
16. The crowd cheered loudly for him.

COMPOUND SUBJECTS AND PREDICATES

- A **compound subject** is two or more subjects that have the same predicate. The subjects in a compound subject are usually joined by a **conjunction**, or connecting word, such as *and* or *or*.

- A **compound predicate** is made up of two or more predicates that have the same subject. The predicates in a compound predicate are usually joined by a conjunction such as *and, but,* or *or.*

- If there are three or more subjects or predicates in a compound subject or predicate, use commas to separate them.

Write the compound subject of each sentence. Then write the conjunction.

1. **Swimming and roller-skating were not Lupe's sports.**

2. **Basketball and baseball weren't either.**

3. **Spelling, chess, and science were Lupe's strengths.**

4. **Lupe and her brother played marbles often.**

5. **Lupe, Rachel, and Yolanda were good marble players.**

6. **The girl or her opponent would win.**

Write the compound predicate of each sentence. Then write the conjunction.

7. **Lupe hopped out of bed and looked in the closet for marbles.**

8. **She smoothed out her bedspread and practiced shooting.**

9. **Lupe flexed and squeezed her thumb.**

10. **She took off her mittens and rubbed her thumb.**

11. **Lupe smiled but said nothing.**

COMPOUND SUBJECTS AND PREDICATES

Combine each group of sentences into one sentence that has a compound subject. Use the conjunction given in parentheses.

1. Her brother lost games to her. Alfonso lost games to her. (and)

2. Skill would be important. A strong thumb would be important. (and)

3. Her brother encouraged her. Her father encouraged her. (and)

4. Rachel might beat her. Yolanda might beat her. Miss Baseball Cap might beat her. (or)

5. Marbles keep Lupe busy. Homework keeps Lupe busy. (and)

6. Her mom wants her to practice basketball. Her dad wants her to practice basketball. (and)

Combine each group of sentences into one sentence that has a compound predicate. Use the conjunction given in parentheses.

7. She played the piano. She did well in chess. (and)

8. Lupe could spell well. Lupe couldn't play soccer. (but)

9. She dumped the marbles onto the bed. She picked five. (and)

10. Miss Baseball Cap might win. Miss Baseball Cap might lose. Miss Baseball Cap might tie the game. (or)

11. Lupe shot hard. Lupe cracked two marbles. (and)

12. Everyone clapped their hands. Everyone hugged her. (and)

CUMULATIVE REVIEW

Write the complete subject. Then write the simple subject.

1. The referee stopped the game.
2. Spectators had gathered too close to the players.
3. The tense and excited players continued the match.

Write the complete predicate. Then write the simple predicate.

4. Lupe missed her next shot.
5. Her opponent tied the game.
6. Only three marbles remained.

Combine each group of sentences into a single sentence with a compound subject or a compound predicate. Use a conjunction that makes sense.

7. Lupe became the spelling bee champion. Lupe won the reading contest three times in a row.
8. She ate dinner with her family. She said nothing about her plans.
9. Her father stared at her. Her mother stared at her.
10. Rachel competed against Lupe. Yolanda competed against Lupe. Miss Baseball Cap competed against Lupe.

SIMPLE AND COMPOUND SENTENCES

Skill Reminder

- A **simple sentence** expresses only one complete thought. The subject or predicate may be simple or compound.
- A **compound sentence** is made up of two or more simple sentences.
- The simple sentences are usually joined by a comma and a **coordinating conjunction**—a connecting word such as *and, or,* or *but.* They also may be connected by a semicolon (;).
- Avoid writing **run-on sentences** (two or more sentences joined as a compound sentence with nothing between them) and **comma splices** (two sentences joined by only a comma and no conjunction).

Write each sentence. Underline the simple sentences that make up each compound sentence. Then circle the conjunction that joins them.

1. Some kids do things well; others mess up.
2. Linda called to Darnell, and he answered her.
3. You put your mind to a problem, and it can be solved.
4. Some people need help, and others can offer it.
5. People heard about Sweeby, and a hospital offered him a job.

Write each compound sentence, correcting any errors. Add punctuation and conjunctions as needed.

6. Darnell wanted to speak at the meeting he was nervous.
7. Darnell finished his speech, Miss Seldes congratulated him.
8. The council members voted, then the meeting was over.
9. We lost you spoke well.

SIMPLE AND COMPOUND SENTENCES

Combine each pair of sentences into a compound sentence. Choose from the box a conjunction that fits each sentence best. Write your sentence.

and	but	or

1. The school board wants a parking lot. Darnell wants a garden.

2. Linda Gold took one side of the issue. Darnell took the other.

3. The hall might be empty. All the seats might be filled.

4. The council could vote for a garden. It could vote for the parking lot.

5. Darnell's article was published. People paid attention to him.

6. The Corner Crew were mostly good kids. No one listened to them.

7. The garden is small. It is a start.

8. You can eat homegrown produce. You can sell it.

9. You may not think about homeless people. They are still there.

CUMULATIVE REVIEW

Read the passage. Choose the best way to write each underlined section. If it is correct, choose *No mistake.*

(1) At the weekly meeting, three items of business. Were discussed. **(2) Zoning violations were discussed first.** **(3) Darnell attended the meeting. Darnell spoke about the gym.** **(4) Everyone listened politely to Linda, Darnell's speech made people respond.**

1. A At the weekly meeting, and three items of business were discussed.

    B At the weekly meeting, when three items of business were discussed.

    C At the weekly meeting, three items of business were discussed.

    D No mistake

2. F Zoning violations were discussed. First.

    G Zoning violations, which were discussed first.

    H Which zoning violations were discussed first.

    J No mistake

3. A Darnell attended the meeting, he spoke about the gym.

    B Darnell attended the meeting and spoke about the gym.

    C Darnell attended the meeting and speaking about the gym.

    D Darnell attended the meeting spoke about the gym.

4. F Everyone listened politely to Linda, but Darnell's speech made people respond.

    G Everyone listened politely to Linda, or Darnell's speech made people respond.

    H Everyone listened politely to Linda Darnell's speech made people respond.

    J No mistake

CLAUSES AND PHRASES

Write the independent clauses in each sentence.

1. The girls cut dolls from old magazines, and the cutouts were used as story characters.

2. The dolls' clothes were out of fashion.

3. The door opened, and Mama followed Kirsti into the room.

4. The girls liked new things, but new things were hard to find.

Identify the dependent and independent clause in each sentence. If the item is a phrase, write *phrase.*

5. Kirsti objected because she disliked green shoes.

6. She was happy when Ellen suggested black.

7. Examining the shoes closely.

8. No one must know about the shoes.

9. Although she liked the black shoes, the green shoes fit better.

CLAUSES AND PHRASES

Write each pair of independent clauses as one sentence by making one independent clause a dependent clause. Use conjunctions from the box below. Conjunctions may be used more than once.

although	when	after	because
before	since	while	

1. Ellen's parents left her with the Johansens. She grew sad.

2. Mama cooked a delicious dinner. It was not a happy evening.

3. The police didn't find the Rosens at home. They searched the Johansens' apartment.

4. Annemarie told Ellen about her sister Lise's death. They went to bed.

5. The police pounded on the door. The girls became frightened.

6. Ellen was afraid. She couldn't get her necklace off.

7. The police entered the bedroom. Annemarie pulled the necklace off Ellen's neck.

8. The police were suspicious. Ellen had dark hair.

CUMULATIVE REVIEW

Write each compound sentence. Underline the simple sentences. Then circle the conjunction that joins them.

1. The Germans had occupied Denmark for almost a year, and many things were in short supply.

2. Leather shoes were no longer in the stores, but people could buy shoes made of fish skin.

3. Germans took lists of names from synagogues in Denmark, and many families were sent away.

Write the compound part of the sentence. Write whether it is a *compound subject* or a *compound predicate*. Then write the conjunction.

4. Annemarie and Ellen acted out scenes with their dolls.

5. The children liked Tivoli and enjoyed the fireworks.

6. The king blew up Danish naval vessels and prevented a German takeover of the navy.

Write the two clauses in each item as one sentence. Use the subordinating conjunction in parentheses.

7. Mrs. Rosen was worried. The Germans might take her family away. (because)

8. Mrs. Rosen asked Mama to take care of Ellen. Mama agreed. (when)

9. Ellen is staying with the Johansens. She may be safe. (because)

10. The Rosens will be "relocated." They are caught. (if)

COMPLEX SENTENCES

- A **complex sentence** consists of an independent clause and at least one dependent clause.

- Dependent clauses often tell *what, when, where, why,* or *which one.*

- A dependent clause that begins a sentence is usually followed by a comma. A dependent clause in the middle of the sentence is set off by commas. A dependent clause at the end of a sentence is usually *not* preceded by a comma.

Write the dependent clause of each sentence. Write whether it describes *what, when, where, why,* or *which one.*

1. **Before "The Early Show" came on, Sara watched game shows.**

2. **She knew the actors' lines because she had heard them so often.**

3. **When one actor said something, Sara joined in with the other actor's reply.**

4. **Charlie is the one who watched television with her.**

5. **Charlie liked to go where Sara went.**

Write each sentence, adding commas where needed. If no punctuation is needed, write *No mistake.*

6. **Because Sara was nearly crying her voice wavered.**

7. **Her eyes followed the trail as she looked down into the valley.**

8. **Charlie when he cried let out a high wail.**

COMPLEX SENTENCES

Write each pair of sentences as one complex sentence, using a conjunction from the box. Not all conjunctions will be used.

after	as	because	if	when
although	before	since	until	while

1. Charlie didn't come home. Neighbors helped in the search.
2. They searched. It grew dark.
3. He didn't know the time of day. Charlie got confused.
4. Sara needed to find Charlie. There was still time.
5. She fell to her knees. She slipped on some dry leaves.
6. He heard Sara. Charlie would shout back.
7. His sister found him. He answered her call.
8. Sara had to lean against a tree. She did not want to fall.
9. Sara saw Charlie. She was relieved.
10. They were together. Charlie and Sara were no longer afraid.

CUMULATIVE REVIEW

Write whether each sentence is *simple*, *compound*, or *complex*.

1. Although the fog was thick, Charlie kept walking through the ravine.
2. When the sun came out, it burned the fog away.
3. He could keep going, or he could just wait for his sister to find him.
4. He sat down on a log and stared straight ahead.
5. He wiped his cheeks where the tears and dirt had dried.

Write each sentence, adding commas where needed. If no punctuation is needed, write *No mistake*. Then underline each dependent clause and write whether it describes *what, when, where, why,* or *which one.*

6. When he was in school Charlie had once gotten lost.
7. He grew frightened because strange children kept looking at him.
8. Because he didn't know the time Charlie got worried.
9. Charlie while he sat on the log looked at his foot.
10. Charlie couldn't remember another time when his watch had stopped.

COMMON AND PROPER NOUNS; ABBREVIATIONS

Identify each common noun and each proper noun.

1. Travis ran up the trail toward the creek.
2. Little Arliss was in the water with a bear.
3. He held the leg of the cub.
4. Travis might not get to his brother quickly.
5. Old Yeller helped rescue Little Arliss.
6. The bear chased Old Yeller.
7. Mama thinks Little Arliss should avoid Birdsong Creek.

COMMON AND PROPER NOUNS; ABBREVIATIONS

Write the abbreviations used in each sentence, and then spell out each abbreviation.

1. Mr. Daniel, the principal, talked to Andrew.

2. Andrew lives on Sullivan St.

3. Dr. Kilmer examined the boy.

4. In his report he wrote, "Cut measures 2 in. long."

5. The report was dated "Fri., Aug. 14."

6. Prof. Arthur Bell is an expert on bears.

Write a proper noun that names a specific example of each common noun. Remember to begin each important word with a capital letter.

7. state

8. city

9. country

10. building

11. friend

12. relative

13. music group

14. continent

15. river

16. ocean

Write your own sentences, using the full words represented by the abbreviations below.

17. mi.

18. Sat.

19. Dr.

20. cm

Washington D.C.

Write each sentence. Underline each independent clause once and each dependent clause twice. Write whether each sentence is *simple*, *compound*, or *complex*.

1. If Mama wanted Little Arliss to kill snakes, he would kill them.
2. The snakes would be dead, but Arliss put them in his pockets.
3. After Old Yeller came along, Arliss caught bigger things.
4. Once, he caught a few rabbits.
5. He caught a baby possum because it played dead.
6. Old Yeller actually caught the animals and brought them to Arliss.

Write each sentence, using lowercase and capital letters to correct any errors in the common and proper nouns.

7. mama asked travis where little Arliss was.
8. travis said his Brother was probably down at birdsong creek.
9. When arliss got cut by the fish fins, mama almost took him to see the Doctor.
10. I told mama that old Yeller was going to make arliss the biggest Liar in all of texas.

SINGULAR AND PLURAL NOUNS

- Most nouns have regular plurals formed by adding *s* or *es* to the singular. For some nouns, the final *y* is changed to *i* before *es* is added.

- Some **irregular nouns** have a special spelling in the plural form. Other irregular nouns have the same spelling for both the singular and the plural.

Write the singular noun in each sentence. Then write each plural noun.

1. The banks of the river were muddy.
2. The dogs jumped over the edge.
3. The men were held only by a rope.
4. A family sat by the windows.

Write each sentence, using the correct plural form of the noun in parentheses.

5. The wet (branch) hung low.
6. Dara Lynn had milk and (cracker).
7. Were any (pony) in the river?
8. The (wife) stayed on the riverbank.

Write two sentences of your own, using the plural form of each noun.

9. goose
10. leaf

SINGULAR AND PLURAL NOUNS

For some nouns ending in *y*, you must add *s* to the singular to form the plural. For others, you must change the *y* to *i* before adding *es*. Match each noun with the rule that tells how to form the plural. Then write the plural form of each noun. The same rule may apply to more than one word.

Rules

a. Add *s*.

b. Change *y* to *i* and add *es*.

1.	key	5.	penny
2.	lady	6.	way
3.	puppy	7.	ferry
4.	toy	8.	duty

Write the plural form of each noun. Use a dictionary to help you if necessary.

9.	city	15.	beagle
10.	ditch	16.	sheep
11.	edge	17.	baby
12.	goose	18.	belief
13.	stomach	19.	wolf
14.	half	20.	sash

CUMULATIVE REVIEW

Write each sentence. Underline each independent clause once and each dependent clause twice. Circle each subordinating conjunction.

1. When Judd got out of the water, someone had a blanket ready.
2. Although Shiloh was shaking from the cold, he licked Marty's face.
3. As Marty picked Shiloh up, he reached out and hugged Judd.
4. After Ma found out, she cried.

Write each common noun and each proper noun.

5. Steady rains had raised the level of the water.
6. Marty and David ran down to Middle Island Creek.
7. Michael Sholt told them to look for a sick man.
8. Mrs. Ellison usually brought a cake.

Write each sentence, using the correct plural form of the noun in parentheses.

9. How many (dummy) are floating in the river?
10. Both its (leg) were stuffed with straw.
11. His (foot) looked strange.
12. Marty planned to give Dara Lynn one of the (kitten).

POSSESSIVE NOUNS

- To form the possessive of most singular nouns, add an apostrophe and *s* ('s).

- To form the possessive of a plural noun that ends in *s*, add only an apostrophe ('). To form the possessive of a plural noun that does not end in *s*, add an apostrophe and *s* ('s).

Write each sentence, using the possessive form of the singular noun in parentheses.

1. The haze in the (earth) atmosphere was thick.
2. The (sun) rays were cut off.
3. A (volcano) eruption caused the problem.
4. The haze affected the (soil) ability to soak up moisture.
5. The (Mississippi) tributaries were full.

Write each sentence, using the possessive form of the plural noun in parentheses.

6. The (cities) concrete walls were strong.
7. The (trees) roots were loosened by the rain.
8. Were the (planters) crops destroyed?
9. The (townspeople) work made a difference.
10. The (men) energy was almost gone.

POSSESSIVE NOUNS

Write the possessive form of the noun in parentheses, and identify it as *singular* or *plural*.

1. The announcer read the (scientist) report.
2. The (engineer) biggest worry was that a levee would break.
3. Even St. Louis was in (harm) way.
4. Acres of the (farmers) crops were flooded.
5. People in Niota appreciated the (prisoners) work.

Write each pair of sentences as one sentence, using possessive nouns to avoid unnecessary repetition.

Example: The woman saw a coat float by. The coat belonged to her son.

    The woman saw her son's coat float by.

6. One girl watched a silo get crushed. The silo belonged to her family.
7. The children saw the results of the work. The work was done by the prisoners.
8. The noise went on all night. The noise was from the bulldozers.
9. In spite of efforts, a levee broke. The efforts were by the workers.
10. The pressure broke through the sandbags. The pressure was from the river current.

CUMULATIVE REVIEW

Choose the best way to write each underlined section. If the underlined section is correct, choose *No mistake*.

It all began after a volcano erupted in the (1) Philippine islands. Because the atmosphere was full of haze, the (2) suns rays could not shine through. (3) That summer of 1992 was cooler than usual, it rained continuously. The water level of the (4) Mississippi river and its tributaries began to rise dangerously.

1. **A** philippine Islands

   B Philippine Islands

   C philippine islands

   D No mistake

2. **F** suns'

   G sun's

   H sunes

   J No mistake

3. **A** That summer of 1992 was cooler than usual, and it rained continuously.

   B That summer of 1992 was cooler than usual it rained continuously.

   C That summer of 1992 was cooler than usual, it raining continuously.

   D No mistake

4. **F** mississippi River

   G Mississippi River

   H mississippi river

   J No mistake

SUBJECT AND OBJECT PRONOUNS

- A **pronoun** takes the place of one or more nouns.

- A pronoun's **number** tells whether it is singular or plural. A pronoun's **gender** tells whether it is masculine, feminine, or neuter.

- The **antecedent** of a pronoun is the noun or nouns to which the pronoun refers. A pronoun must agree with its antecedent in number and gender.

- **Subject pronouns** *(I, you, he, she, it, we, they)* replace the subject of a sentence. **Object pronouns** *(me, you, him, her, it, us, them)* replace a noun after an action verb, such as *see* or *tell*, or after a preposition, such as *to* or *with*.

Write each sentence. Underline the pronoun and circle the antecedent. Then write whether the pronoun is *singular* or *plural* and *masculine, feminine,* or *neuter.*

1. **The young girl's wolf cub barked at her.**

2. **A wolf has sharp senses and uses them to hunt.**

Write each sentence, using the pronoun form in parentheses that best completes the sentence.

3. **Sean showed (I, me) the book, and (I, me) liked (it, them).**

4. **(He, Him) will copy the map of migrations for Sarah and (I, me).**

5. **(She and I, Her and me) should read more about (they, them).**

6. **Sarah says the study of early humans interests (she, her).**

7. **(We, Us) are working on a project about the migrations.**

SUBJECT AND OBJECT PRONOUNS

Write each sentence, replacing the word or words in parentheses with a pronoun. Then write whether the pronoun is a *subject* pronoun or an *object* pronoun.

1. Humans stopped roaming because (humans) began to grow grain for food.

2. Sources of water were scarce, and people had to stay near (sources of water).

3. The woman is walking to the field where (the woman) grows wheat.

4. That man is carrying a heavy basket; perhaps another person should help (that man).

Write each sentence, replacing the word or words in parentheses with the correct pronoun. Then write the antecedent.

5. The woman uses a knife as (she, her) removes the seeds from the stalk heads.

6. When seeds were dropped on the ground, (they, them) would sprout.

7. Grain could be stored all winter until the people needed (it, them) for food.

8. People knew that grain would feed (they, them) during the winter.

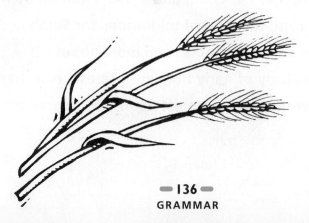

CUMULATIVE REVIEW

Write the correct possessive for each word in parentheses.

1. (Sasha) father tamed the wolf cubs.
2. The cubs joined in the (children) games.
3. The wolves copied their (owners) expressions.
4. The (family) new pets even helped them hunt.

Write the correct plural form of each noun.

5. group
6. bush
7. moose
8. family

Write each sentence, choosing the correct subject or object pronoun in parentheses.

9. The mother wolf was very ill, so (she, her) abandoned the two cubs.
10. Sasha found (they, them) near the ravine.
11. (She, Her) called her brother over and showed (he, him) the cubs.
12. Sasha named one cub Tiki, and (she, her) named the other one Taki.
13. When Sasha's brother called the cubs, (them, they) ran to (he, him).

POSSESSIVE PRONOUNS

Write the possessive pronoun of each sentence. If the possessive pronoun is used before a noun, write the noun also.

1. Early Chinese emperors gave huge estates to their friends.

2. Emperor Qin Shi Huang Di began the Great Wall of China to protect his borders from invasion.

3. Can you imagine spending your life building a wall?

4. That travel brochure is mine.

5. Is this map of China yours?

Write each sentence, choosing the correct pronoun or contraction in parentheses.

6. When will you leave on (your, you're) trip?

7. (It's, Its) an exciting opportunity to learn more about China.

8. The Harrigans wanted (they're, their) trip to last forever.

9. (They're, Their) going back again next summer.

POSSESSIVE PRONOUNS

Write each sentence, replacing the word or words in parentheses with the appropriate possessive pronoun.

1. (Cheung's and my) class is making a display about the Chinese system of terraces.

2. We are learning about China and (China's) exciting history.

3. The Chinese people had to irrigate (the Chinese people's) land in order to grow good crops.

4. That drawing of the farmer plowing (the farmer's) field is mine.

5. Li and David used yarn and glue to make (Li and David's) model.

6. Sandra worked with colored paper to make (Sandra's).

7. Ann, did you complete (Ann's) part of the project?

8. My idea may have worked, Cheung, but I like (Cheung's) better.

CUMULATIVE REVIEW

Write each sentence, replacing the word or words in parentheses with the correct pronoun.

1. Julia and (I, me) went to the library.
2. (We, Us) are doing a report about ancient China.
3. I helped (she, her) find a book about the early emperors.
4. Julia will write the section about (they, them).

Write each sentence, using the conjunction that correctly completes the sentence.

5. Cheung types well, (but, or) Marla does not.
6. The report is due next week, (or, and) they have to choose a topic.
7. They may write about the Great Wall, (or, and) they may do research on the invention of paper instead.

Write each sentence, choosing the pronoun or contraction in parentheses that correctly completes the sentence.

8. Do you know which topic you will use for (your, you're) report?
9. (My, Mine) will be on Chinese writing.
10. Did Jennifer finish (her, hers) report on the Forbidden City?

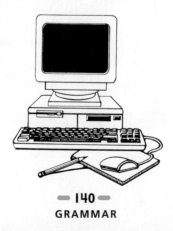

CASE; REFLEXIVE PRONOUNS

- The **case** of a pronoun shows how it is used in a sentence: subjective case—*I, you, she, he, it, we, they;* objective case—*me, you, her, him, it, us, them;* possessive case—*my/mine, your/yours, her/hers, his, its, our/ours, their/theirs.*

- The **reflexive pronoun** *(myself, yourself, herself, himself, itself, ourselves, yourselves, themselves)* usually refers to the subject of a sentence. A reflexive pronoun should not be used as the subject.

Write each sentence, using the pronoun that correctly completes the sentence. Then write whether each pronoun is *subjective, objective,* or *possessive.*

1. Many Egyptian pyramids have the same shape, but (they, them, their) sizes vary greatly.

2. To bring the heavy stones from the quarry, workers transported (they, them, themselves) in wooden boats along the Nile.

3. Imhotep designed Egypt's first pyramid; (it, its, itself) is known as the Step Pyramid.

4. A pyramid would be built close to the pharaoh's palace so that he could see (it, they, them).

Write the reflexive pronoun used in each sentence. Then write its antecedent.

5. Manuel, try this project yourself.

6. Sheila poured herself a glass of water.

7. Nancy and Marissa cooked an Egyptian meal by themselves.

CASE; REFLEXIVE PRONOUNS

Complete the following story by writing the word in parentheses that best completes each sentence.

The two workers sat side by side, thinking to (1) (themself, themselves, theirselves). Queen Ashkena had asked (2) (them, they, themselves) to carve a statue for (3) (she, her, hers) in time for tomorrow's feast.

"Naator and (4) (me, myself, I) have been working on this stone for two weeks," thought Moshe, "and (5) (they, us, it) still isn't ready. What will the queen say when (6) (she, her, herself) finds out?"

(7) (Him, He, His) looked at (8) (him, he, his) friend. "(9) (We, Us, Ourselves) need a plan. The other carvers are finished with (10) (their, there, they're) work and have already begun to arrive for the feast. Queen Ashkena will be very disappointed in (11) (we, us, our) when the pharaoh tells (12) (she, her, hers) that (13) (we, us, our) statue isn't ready."

Naator looked up. The pharaoh was walking toward (14) (he, they, them)! "Are (15) (you, yours, yourselves) finished with the statue?" (16) (him, he, his) asked. (17) "(Me, My, Mine) wife is eager to see (18) (it, them, they)."

"Of course!" Naator exclaimed. "(19) (It, Them, They) will be at the palace tomorrow at dawn."

After the pharaoh had left, Moshe stared at (20) (him, he, his) friend. "What do (21) (yours, your, you) have to say for (22) (yourself, yourselves, you)? There isn't enough time for two men to finish that statue before dawn!"

"(23) (You're, Your, Youre) right," said Naator. "But look! The other carvers are coming over to help (24) (ourselves, us, our)!"

CUMULATIVE REVIEW

Write each sentence, using the pronoun that correctly completes the sentence. Then write whether each sentence is *declarative*, *interrogative*, *imperative*, or *exclamatory*.

1. Do you know how (they, them) moved those gigantic stones?

2. They used ramps to help bring the stones to (their, theirs) destination.

3. I see a tour guide; let's ask (her, hers) how it was done.

4. What a clever idea; I wish it had been (my, mine)!

5. Tell me about (your, yours) idea.

Write each sentence, replacing the word or words in parentheses with a reflexive pronoun.

6. Janette and Al treated (Janette and Al) to a movie.

7. Janette bought popcorn for (Janette).

8. Al bought (Al) some peanut butter crackers.

9. The two friends divided the refreshments between (the two friends).

ADJECTIVES AND ARTICLES

- An **adjective** modifies, or describes, a noun or a pronoun. Adjectives can tell *what kind, how many,* or *which one.*

- The adjectives *a, an,* and *the* are called **articles**. *The* refers to a particular person, place, thing, or idea. *A* and *an* refer to any person, place, thing, or idea.

- Use *a* before a consonant and *an* before a vowel sound.

Write the adjective or adjectives used in each sentence. Write whether each adjective describes *what kind, how many,* or *which one*. Do not write articles.

1. Researchers have uncovered many artifacts.

2. Diggers found enormous gardens.

3. One room was for bathing.

4. Several homes were luxurious.

5. Lava and ash covered all buildings.

Write each sentence, using the article that correctly completes the sentence.

6. Have you ever taken (a, an) trip to Greece?

7. Have you studied (an, the) classical period of Greek history?

8. (A, The) Greeks built temples of stone.

9. (An, The) map shows Athens and Sparta.

10. Crete is (a, an) island off the coast of Greece.

ADJECTIVES AND ARTICLES

Write each sentence, supplying an article for the blank. Underline each adjective and write whether it describes *what kind, how many,* or *which one.*

1. Rome was once _____ cluster of tribal settlements.

2. _____ million people lived in Rome.

3. What _____ crowded city it must have been!

4. It was _____ largest city in the world.

5. Its emperor was _____ powerful ruler.

6. Its roads formed _____ vast network.

7. Was it _____ first city to use aqueducts?

8. _____ aqueducts they built carried clean water to cities.

9. Romans liked to visit _____ public baths.

10. _____ houses in town often had beautiful gardens.

CUMULATIVE REVIEW

Write the pronoun in parentheses that correctly completes each sentence. Then write whether the pronoun is a *subject, object, possessive,* or *reflexive* pronoun.

1. The Greeks made (their, theirs) public buildings out of stone and marble.
2. Many of (they, them) were temples to gods and goddesses.
3. Pericles led Athens in the war against Sparta; (he, himself) was a great leader.
4. Because Athens was a democracy, Athenians could choose new leaders for (theirselves, themselves).

Write each sentence, replacing the noun in parentheses with the correct possessive form. Include any articles, if necessary—for example, *the Trojans'.*

5. (Homer) new poem is about Odysseus.
6. (Greeks) war with Troy is described in another poem.
7. (goddess) name was Athena.
8. (Greeks) love of drama is well known.
9. Smiles and frowns were shown by (actors) masks.
10. (temple) shape and size are pleasing.

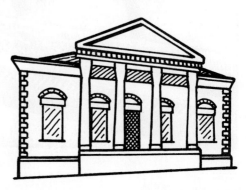

PROPER AND DEMONSTRATIVE ADJECTIVES

Skill Reminder

- **Proper adjectives** are formed from proper nouns and are always capitalized.

- Proper adjectives are formed in a variety of ways. If you are not sure how to form a particular proper adjective, look in a dictionary.

- A **demonstrative adjective** points out a noun and tells *which one*. The words *this, that, these,* and *those* are demonstrative adjectives.

Spain/Spanish	Egypt/Egyptian
China/Chinese	Greece/Greek
Sweden/Swedish	Venezuela/Venezuelan
Vietnam/Vietnamese	Israel/Israeli

1.–5. Choose proper adjectives from the chart above to write five sentences of your own. You may use the proper noun as well, if you wish.

Write each demonstrative adjective.

6. I want you to examine these coins carefully.

7. Can you read the letters on this inscription?

8. That temple was built in honor of Athena.

9. Millions of people have climbed the Acropolis to see those ruins.

PROPER AND DEMONSTRATIVE ADJECTIVES

Write the proper adjective that corresponds to each proper noun. Use a dictionary if you are not sure of the adjective form.

1. Paris
2. England
3. France
4. Belgium
5. Africa
6. Denmark
7. Pakistan
8. Milan
9. America
10. Canada

Write each sentence, using the correct form of the demonstrative adjective in parentheses. Then underline each proper adjective.

11. (That) playwright is Greek.
12. (This) old Spanish coins are valuable.
13. I saw (that) Lebanese tablecloths in a museum.
14. Don't you think (this) Irish lace is beautiful?
15. Taste (this) French cheese.
16. May I wear (that) Mexican sombrero?

CUMULATIVE REVIEW

Read the passage and choose the word that belongs where each number is.

I just read a play that takes place in ancient Greece. The main character is Pericles, an (1) general. One of (2) skills is public speaking. He is also known for (3) wisdom. Pericles is looking for (4) particular person. (5) person must have a special skill. Whoever is chosen receives (6) award.

Everyone has a particular skill. I think I know what (7) is. What is (8)?

1. Athenian
   athens
   athenian
   Athens

2. his's
   His
   his
   he's

3. His
   his
   his's
   he's

4. a
   an
   the
   these

5. these
   That
   Those
   These

6. a
   an
   the
   these

7. mine
   my
   myself
   me

8. you're
   your's
   your
   yours

COMPARING WITH ADJECTIVES

- To form the **comparative** of most one-syllable adjectives, add *er*. For most adjectives of two or more syllables, add the word *more* before the adjective.

- To form the **superlative** of most one-syllable adjectives, add *est.* For most adjectives of two or more syllables, add the word *most*.

- To indicate that something does not have as much of a quality, use *less* and *least* with most adjectives.

- Some adjectives have special forms for comparing:

good, better, best	much, more, most
well (healthy), better, best	many, more, most
bad, worse, worst	little, less, least

Write the form of the adjective in parentheses that best completes each sentence.

1. The reeds are (strong) than twine.

2. These flowers are the (fragrant) ones in the garden.

3. That insect is (small) than an ant.

4. The (tiresome) task of all was hollowing out the trunk.

Write the correct form of the adjective in parentheses.

5. Those nuts had the (bad) flavor I've ever tasted.

6. The berries tasted (good) than the nuts.

7. Building a fire took (much) effort than we thought it would.

8. The rocks were the (good) place of all to make a fire.

COMPARING WITH ADJECTIVES

Write the comparative and superlative forms of each word.

1. high
2. clear
3. inviting
4. magnificent
5. good or well
6. bad

Each sentence has an adjective error. Write each sentence, using the correct adjective form.

7. This number of birds is the many I've ever seen.
8. The weather this spring is gooder than it was last year.
9. We had much snow last year than this year.
10. Last month there was least sleet and rain than this month.
11. This is the worsest winter we've ever had.
12. We spent little time hiking than doing chores.

CUMULATIVE REVIEW

Write each sentence, using the correct word of the two in parentheses.

1. After the crow landed, (it, its) cawed loudly.
2. (That, Those) animals are eating some food.
3. Try to guess the weight of (this, these) big stone.
4. The biggest stone looks like a (Greece, Greek) statue.
5. The boy cooked a very nice meal for (hisself, himself).
6. He used an old (Mexican, Mexico) recipe.

Write each sentence, using the correct form of the adjective in parentheses.

7. This is the (good) hickory nut I've ever tasted.
8. I think violets are (nice) than bluebells.
9. Are violets the (attractive) flowers of all?
10. That is the (big) squirrel I've ever seen.
11. Our rose bush has produced (pretty) flowers than last year.
12. This book is the (interesting) one of the series.

MAIN AND HELPING VERBS

- A verb that includes two or more words is a **verb phrase.** The **main verb** is the most important verb in a verb phrase.

- A **helping verb** works with the main verb. Forms of *be, have, do, can, will, may,* and *shall* can be used as helping verbs. A main verb can have more than one helping verb.

- The form of the verb changes to agree in number with the subject of the sentence. This is called **subject-verb agreement.**

Write the verb phrase used in each sentence. Then write the main verb.

1. Febold is living alone on the Great Plains.
2. He had lived by himself for a year.
3. He did not have any neighbors.
4. Many wagon trains were passing his house.
5. The pioneers must be going to California for gold.

Write each sentence, using the verb form in parentheses that agrees with the subject.

6. The wagon trains (is, are) heading west.
7. (Was, Were) the pioneers looking for gold?
8. Febold (has, have) thought of an idea.
9. Olaf (was, were) thinking about the fog.
10. Every frog in the field (is, are) croaking loudly.

MAIN AND HELPING VERBS

Write the verb phrase used in each sentence. Then write the main verb.

1. Most farmers would want open, flat land.
2. The cows will be enjoying the abundant pastures.
3. The pioneers might listen to Febold.
4. They could talk about the long growing season.
5. The warm, sunny days will produce large crops.

Write each sentence. Supply a helping verb in place of the missing word.

6. Many pioneers ____ traveled west.
7. Febold ____ seen them every day in their wagons.
8. Febold ____ hoping for a miracle.
9. People ____ looking at the fog.
10. ____ that cloud moving away from the fog?

Write each sentence, using the subject shown in parentheses. Change the verb form to agree with the new subject.

11. A pioneer was dipping pans into the water. (Two pioneers)
12. Olaf is stumbling toward the wagon. (Olaf and Anna)
13. The pioneers have learned to make postholes. (Febold)

Write each sentence, using the correct form of the adjective in parentheses.

1. **This frog is very (loud).**
2. **It is (wet) now than it was before.**
3. **That is the (cute) frog I've ever seen.**
4. **That frog seems (happy) than this one.**
5. **Of all the frogs here, that one has the (interesting) croak.**

Write each sentence, supplying a helping verb.

6. **A tall man ____ standing by the road.**
7. **Many wagons ____ passed by.**
8. **Some people ____ stopping.**
9. **Febold ____ not know any of them.**
10. **He ____ shouting.**
11.–12. Think of an adjective. Then write two sentences. Write one sentence using the comparative form of that adjective and one using the superlative form.

ACTION VERBS; OBJECTS OF VERBS

Skill Reminder

- The noun or pronoun that receives the action of the verb is the **direct object**.

- An **indirect object** tells to whom or what, or for whom or what, the action of the verb is done. Verbs that may take indirect objects include *ask, send, tell, get, buy, show, do,* and *make.*

- A verb that has a direct object is sometimes called a **transitive verb**. A verb that has no direct object is sometimes called an **intransitive verb**.

Write each sentence, adding an indirect object. Underline direct objects once and indirect objects twice in each sentence you write.

1. **Frank made a strawberry milkshake.**

2. **Gerald sold some lemonade.**

3. **Milton Reynolds showed his pen.**

4. **Johnson & Johnson gave free bandages.**

5. **Levi Strauss sent some jeans.**

Write the verb or verb phrase used in each sentence. Tell whether it is *transitive* or *intransitive*. If it is transitive, write the direct object.

6. **Mr. Pascal looked all over.**

7. **He found his son's box.**

8. **Sixteen dials covered the top.**

9. **Mr. Pascal laughed.**

10. **Blaise's invention might win a prize.**

ACTION VERBS; OBJECTS OF VERBS

Write the verb or verb phrase used in each sentence. Tell whether it is *transitive* or *intransitive*. If it is transitive, write the direct object.

1. The miners worked hard.
2. They needed tough pants.
3. Levi stitched overalls out of tent canvas.
4. He showed them to the miners.
5. The overalls were becoming popular.
6. Levi tried a different material.
7. This material was strong but soft.
8. He had dyed it indigo blue.

Write each sentence, adding a direct object or an indirect object in place of the missing word. Then tell whether the word is a *direct object* or an *indirect object*.

9. The teacher gave ____ an assignment.
10. I have made ____ a sketch.
11. Maybe you can give me some other ____.
12. Our librarian loaned us some wonderful ____.
13. I will send ____ a photo of the invention.
14. I should give ____ a name.

CUMULATIVE REVIEW

Write each sentence, using the kind of adjective called for in parentheses.

1. The electric flowerpot was a very (what kind) invention.
2. I would be surprised if the inventor sold (how many) flowerpots.
3. The lightbulb illuminated a(n) (what kind) plant.
4. Do you think that was the inventor's (which one) creation?

Write each sentence, using the form of the helping verb in parentheses that agrees with the subject.

5. Barbara (is, are) snipping pictures of women out of a fashion magazine.
6. She and her mother (was, were) creating a teenage fashion doll.
7. They (has, have) found many beautiful outfits.
8. The doll (do, does) need a name.

Write the direct object and the indirect object of each sentence. Then tell whether each is a *direct object* or an *indirect object.*

9. My friend gave me an idea.
10. She was drinking a root-beer float.
11. I'll make her a chocolate milkshake.
12. Will she like it?

LINKING VERBS

- A **linking verb** links the subject of a sentence to a noun, a pronoun, or an adjective in the predicate. Linking verbs include forms of *be,* as well as the verbs *appear, become, feel, grow, look, seem, smell, sound,* and *taste.* Some of these verbs may be action verbs as well.

- A **predicate nominative** is a noun or pronoun that follows a linking verb and renames the subject. A **predicate adjective** is an adjective that follows a linking verb and describes the subject.

Write the verb used in each sentence. Then tell whether it is used as a *linking verb* or an *action verb.*

1. The air near the bay smelled salty.

2. Mari smelled the flowers nearby.

3. Mrs. Frank felt the clay fish.

4. The homemade clay felt smooth.

Write each sentence, using an example of the word in parentheses to complete the sentence.

5. The bird in Mari's diorama was an (predicate nominative).

6. The osprey's favorite food is (predicate nominative).

7. The fish in the diorama looked (predicate adjective).

8. The main ingredient in the homemade clay was (predicate nominative).

9. Some of the other dioramas seemed (predicate adjective).

10. Because she won first place, Mari felt (predicate adjective).

LINKING VERBS

Write each sentence, adding a linking verb from the box. Not all verbs in the box will be used. Do not use any verb more than once.

appeared	became	felt	grew	looked
seemed	smelled	was	tasted	sounded

1. The subject of Mari's diorama ____ Biscayne Bay.
2. To Mari, the other students' projects ____ better than hers.
3. Only her diorama ____ homemade.
4. Of course, somebody else's project actually ____ fishy!
5. Mari ____ nervous and self-conscious.
6. After winning, however, she ____ very proud of her work.

7.–9. Write three sentences of your own. For each sentence, use any linking verb from the box above. Complete the sentence with a predicate nominative or a predicate adjective.

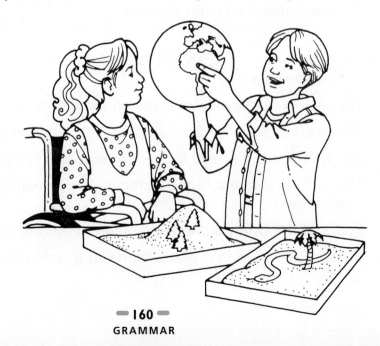

CUMULATIVE REVIEW

Write each sentence, using the correct form of the article in parentheses.

1. At the library, Mari opened (a, an) heavy dictionary.
2. She needed to find (a, an) definition for *diorama.*
3. Mrs. Frank had some photos in (a, an) album.
4. One of the dioramas showed (a, an) ocean scene.

Write each sentence. Circle the action verb or verb phrase in each sentence. Underline each direct object once. Underline each indirect object twice.

5. Mrs. Frank gave Mari some books.
6. Mari asked her mother a question.
7. Mamá dried her hands.
8. She could not buy Mari any supplies.
9. Mari found shells at the beach.
10. Mamá gave Mari a cup of sand.

Write the linking verb used in each sentence. Then write whether the sentence includes a *predicate nominative* or a *predicate adjective.*

11. My little brother is an artist.
12. His drawings of animals are delightful.
13. The shark in this picture looks real.
14. His favorite book is the animal encyclopedia.
15. The pages feel worn.

SIMPLE TENSES; PRESENT TENSE

- The **present tense** of a verb shows that the action is happening now or that it happens over and over.

Present Tense for Regular Verbs

Singular Subjects (*he*, *she*, *it*, or a singular noun)	Rule
most verbs	Add *s*.
verbs ending in *s, ss, sh, ch, x, z*	Add *es*.
verbs ending in consonant + *y*	Change *y* to *i* and add *es*.

Present Tense for *Be* and *Have*

Subject	Forms of *Be*	Forms of *Have*
I	am	have
he, she, it, or a singular noun	is	has
we, you, they, or a plural noun	are	have

For each sentence, write the correct present-tense form of the verb in parentheses.

1. The young man (wave) to the blacksmith.
2. He (carry) some metal over to him.
3. The blacksmith (pass) him a finished piece.
4. The workers (have) new electric arc welders.
5. The tools (be) a great help to him.
6. John (look) at the iron gate.

SIMPLE TENSES; PRESENT TENSE

Write each sentence, using the correct present-tense verb form in parentheses.

1. One of Simmons's most famous pieces (is, are) a bird.

2. Some works (takes, take) him a long time.

3. He (rely, relies) on help from apprentices.

4. Each piece (has, have) an original design.

5. He (spend, spends) many hours on each sketch.

6. Simmons (sketches, sketch) every piece ahead of time.

7.–10. Write four sentences of your own, using singular subjects and different present-tense verbs.

CUMULATIVE REVIEW

Read the passage, and choose the word or group of words that fits best in each numbered space.

Philip Simmons (1) a famous blacksmith. He (2) in South Carolina. A woman asks (3) some questions as he (4) iron bars into amazing forms. The metal bars feel (5). Simmons is skilled in the art of working metal. Just look at (6) newest piece!

1. A be
   B are
   C is
   D were

2. F live
   G living
   H have living
   J lives

3. A he
   B him
   C his
   D himself

4. F bend
   G bendes
   H bends
   J are bending

5. A heavy
   B heavily
   C heavyer
   D heavying

6. F he's
   G his
   H him
   J his's

PAST AND FUTURE TENSES

- To form the **past tense** of most verbs, add *ed* or *d*. If a verb ends with a consonant + *y*, change *y* to *i* and add *ed*. If a verb ends in a stressed syllable with the consonant-vowel-consonant pattern or if a one-syllable verb has this pattern, double the final consonant and add *ed*.

- To form the **future tense** of a verb, use the helping verb *will* with the main verb.

Write the past and future tense of each verb.

1. **destroy**
2. **ban**
3. **occur**
4. **worry**
5. **learn**
6. **bother**

Write each sentence, using the past-tense form of the verb in parentheses.

7. **Students (hurry) down the hall.**
8. **The water fountain never (turn) off.**
9. **Michael's upper lip (quiver).**
10. **Victor (prefer) a smile to a scowl.**
11. **Teresa (smile) at Victor.**

PAST AND FUTURE TENSES

Match each verb with the rule that tells how to form the past tense.
Write the letter of your answer. Then write the past-tense form of
the verb.

> a. Add *ed.*
> b. Change *y* to *i* and add *ed.*
> c. Double the final consonant and add *ed.*

1. mar
2. weather
3. recur
4. profit
5. fatten
6. knot
7. carry
8. refit
9. hurry

Write each sentence, using the verb and tense given in parentheses.

10. When the teacher spoke, he (use; past) only French words.

11. Beginning tomorrow, all students (reply; future) in French.

12. When Mr. Lucas asked for a proper noun, Victor (mention; past)
    Teresa's name.

13. As he sat in math class, Victor (hope; past) he would not be
    called on.

CUMULATIVE REVIEW

Write each sentence, using the correct plural form in parentheses.

1. How many (classes, classes') are you taking?
2. The cafeteria served many (lunchies, lunches) each day.
3. The health class was studying about (dairys, dairies).
4. In his French book, Victor found pictures of (mouses, mice) and cats.

Write the form of the verb in parentheses that agrees with the subject.

5. Victor and Teresa (is, are) in the same French class.
6. In homeroom, Teresa (sit, sits) two rows in front of Victor.
7. On the first day of school, every student (want, wants) to get to the first class.
8. When the bell rings, the students (rush, rushes) down the hall.

Write each sentence, using the correct tense of the verb in parentheses.

9. Victor hopes he (sit) next to Teresa in French class.
10. Maybe she (like) him if he smiles.
11. Victor (pretend) he already knew some French.
12. Mr. Bueller kindly said nothing, so Teresa (believe) him.

PRINCIPAL PARTS OF VERBS

- The **principal parts** of a verb are the *infinitive*, the *present participle*, the *past*, and the *past participle*.
- Participles are used with helping verbs in verb phrases.

INFINITIVE	PRESENT PARTICIPLE	PAST	PAST PARTICIPLE
to walk	walking	walked	walked
to pat	patting	patted	patted
to love	loving	loved	loved
to fry	frying	fried	fried

Write the present participle and the past participle of each verb.

1. **try**
2. **hope**
3. **prefer**
4. **dance**
5. **cough**
6. **bat**

Write each sentence, using the verb and principal part in parentheses.

7. **Maria (plan; present participle) a concert soon.**
8. **Tears (appear; past) in Maria's eyes.**
9. **Maria had (solo; past participle) many times.**

PRINCIPAL PARTS OF VERBS

Write each sentence, using the principal part of the verb in parentheses that fits best.

1. The girls have (form) a group.

2. They are (call) themselves "The Fours."

3. The group is (perform) at Evergreen Residential Manor today.

4. Maria's mother is (videotape) the performance.

5. Mkiwa is (plan) to try an African dance.

6. Mrs. Winters is (arrange) the seats for the audience.

7. The girls have (enjoy) their work together.

8. Jessie has (stop) the applause and is (talk) to the audience.

9. She is (announce) Maria Hernandez, the first performer.

10. Each girl has (commit) herself and is (perform) with great feeling.

11.–12. Using a verb of your choice, write two sentences. Use the present-participle form of the verb in one, and the past-participle form of the verb in the other.

CUMULATIVE REVIEW

Write the sentences. Underline each direct object once and each indirect object twice.

1. Jessie bit her lip.
2. Maria gave Julie her crutch.
3. Jamar asked her a question.
4. Will she perform the leading role?
5. Mkiwa handed Maria some tissues.

Write each sentence, using the past-tense form of the verb in parentheses.

6. The committee (post) the results of the audition.
7. Jessie (worry) because her name wasn't on the list.
8. She (cry) softly as she ran down the hall.
9. Maria (prefer) a solo part in the winter concert.
10. Everyone (wait) for Julie to speak.

Write each sentence, using the verb and form given in parentheses.

11. The manager has (ask; past participle) the girls to do a program.
12. Mkiwa is (wrap; present participle) her head with a scarf.
13. She (dance; future) to drum rhythms.
14. Maria's mother is (lead; present participle) the cheers.

REGULAR AND IRREGULAR VERBS

- The past tense and the past participle of **regular verbs** are formed by adding *d* or *ed*.
- The past tense and the past participle of **irregular verbs** are not formed by adding *d* or *ed*. They are formed in several other ways.

fly, flew, flown	catch, caught, caught
choose, chose, chosen	drink, drank, drunk
tear, tore, torn	be, was/were, been

Write the past tense and the past participle of each verb.

1. grow
2. bear
3. ring
4. freeze
5. lose

Write each sentence, using the verb and form given in parentheses.

6. The point of the stylus had (wear; past participle) down.
7. Dots (swim; past tense) in his mind.
8. Louis's mother wondered whether he had (drink; past participle) his milk.
9. Louis has (choose; past participle) a different dot pattern for each letter.
10. Louis (catch; past tense) a bad cold at school.

REGULAR AND IRREGULAR VERBS

GROUP	VERBS
1	fly, grow
2	tear, wear
3	begin, drink, ring, swim
4	break, choose, freeze
5	bring, catch

The chart above shows some irregular verbs you have learned, listed in similar groups. For each of the following verbs, write the number of the group into which the verb fits.

1. **sink, sank, sunk**

2. **steal, stole, stolen**

3. **blow, blew, blown**

4. **teach, taught, taught**

5. **swear, swore, sworn**

6. **think, thought, thought**

Write each sentence. Use either the past tense or the past participle of the verb in parentheses, depending on which fits the sentence better. Then write *past* or *past participle* to identify the form you chose.

7. **Louis has (bring) his board and stylus.**

8. **Has the teacher (choose) the poem?**

9. **The audience (begin) to arrive.**

10. **Everyone (catch) the excitement of Louis's discovery.**

CUMULATIVE REVIEW

Write the name of the principal part of the underlined verb.

1. Louis's mother <u>worried</u> about him.
2. Louis <u>has walked</u> along the road.
3. He <u>is punching</u> dots into the paper.
4. He <u>had developed</u> an entirely new system.

Write each sentence, using the correct verb form in parentheses.

5. Louis (is, are) sitting on the edge of his bed.
6. Dots (was, were) dancing in Louis's head.
7. Louis (stay, stays) up late.
8. He often (fall, falls) asleep in class.

Write each sentence, using either the past tense or the past participle of the verb in parentheses, depending on which is needed.

9. Monique (fly) up the stairs.
10. Louis's cough has (grow) worse.
11. Louis (catch) people's attention.
12. Has he (begin) writing yet?

PERFECT TENSES

- The **present perfect tense**, formed with *has* or *have* and the past participle of the main verb, shows that the action began sometime before the present. The action may still be going on.

- The **past perfect tense**, formed with *had* and the past participle of the main verb, shows that the action happened before a specific time in the past.

- The **future perfect tense**, formed with *will have* and the past participle of the main verb, shows that the action will have happened before a specific time in the future.

Write the verb phrase used in each sentence. Then write whether it is *present perfect, past perfect,* or *future perfect.*

1. Before next Friday, Marilla and Matthew will have adopted a girl.

2. Anne has been at the orphanage a long time.

3. In the past, Mrs. Lynde had criticized Anne's looks.

4. By tomorrow, Anne will have forgotten about that.

Write the correct form of the verb and tense given in parentheses.

5. The Cuthberts (choose; present perfect) to adopt Anne.

6. Anne (learn; past perfect) many things at the orphanage.

7. Anne (grow; present perfect) taller while living with the Cuthberts.

8. Marilla (cook; past perfect) a stew for last night's dinner.

9. By tomorrow, Anne and Diana (visit; future perfect) each other.

PERFECT TENSES

Write each sentence, replacing the underlined verb with the tense given in parentheses.

1. Anne <u>looked</u> unhappy at the orphanage. (past perfect)
2. She <u>brought</u> several books with her. (present perfect)
3. Marilla <u>wants</u> a boy. (past perfect)
4. Diana <u>talks</u> with many people at the picnic. (future perfect)
5. The afternoon <u>passes</u> so quickly! (present perfect)
6. Anne and Diana <u>took</u> an oath of friendship. (present perfect)
7. Diana <u>invites</u> Anne to the picnic. (present perfect)
8. Soon they <u>will taste</u> the ice cream. (future perfect)
9. Anne <u>will enjoy</u> all of the food at the picnic. (present perfect)
10. Anne <u>touched</u> Marilla's brooch. (past perfect)

CUMULATIVE REVIEW

Write each sentence, using the verb and tense given in parentheses.

1. Anne (arrive; future) at the station at 3:00.
2. By tomorrow, Marilla and Matthew (discuss; future perfect) the matter.
3. Marilla (agree; present perfect) to let Anne stay.
4. Anne (grow; present perfect) comfortable at Green Gables.
5. She (swim; past perfect) in the lake before.
6. Marilla (invite; past) the minister to tea.
7. Who (lose; present perfect) the brooch?
8. The Cuthberts (bring; present perfect) Anne to the picnic.
9. Anne (measure; past perfect) the ingredients carefully.
10. Anne (use; present) cough syrup instead of vanilla.
11. By now, everyone (taste; future perfect) the cake.

PROGRESSIVE FORMS

- **Progressive forms** of verbs tell about action that continues over time.

- Progressive forms are made up of a form of the verb *be* and the present participle of the main verb.

  Present Progressive: She **is riding** now.
  Past Progressive: She **was riding** yesterday.
  Future Progressive: She **will be riding** tomorrow.

Write each sentence, using the correct form of the verb and tense given in parentheses.

1. The cowboys (move; present progressive) the cattle slowly.

2. One cow (wander; past progressive) off.

3. Many (sleep; future progressive) under trees.

4. Some (hide; past progressive) their calves.

5. Who (lead; present progressive) the herd now?

6. Two cowboys (chase; past progressive) a yearling.

Write each sentence, using the form of *be* that fits best.

7. The cowboys (is, are) heading back now.

8. Two hours ago, that man (was, were) chasing two cows.

9. Tomorrow they (will be, were) rounding up more cattle.

10. That cowboy (will be, was) riding with us yesterday.

PROGRESSIVE FORMS

Write each sentence, using the progressive form that corresponds to the tense of the underlined verb.

Example: The cow <u>drank</u>.
The cow was drinking.

1. The cowboy <u>tries</u> to keep the cows together.
2. Colter and Leedro <u>rode</u> together.
3. The drive <u>will begin</u> soon.
4. The cowboys <u>lead</u> the cattle to the pen.
5. Leedro <u>filled</u> his canteen with water.
6. The horses <u>drank</u> thirstily.
7. The windmill <u>turned</u> day and night.
8. The Ebys <u>run</u> seventeen windmills.
9. The cattle <u>struggle</u> to survive.
10. The windmill <u>will pump</u> enough water.

CUMULATIVE REVIEW

Read the passage. Choose the word or group of words that should replace the underlined words. If underlined words are correct, choose *No mistake*

The cowboy (1) <u>will be ride</u> out soon. They (2) <u>are put</u> saddles on (3) <u>them</u> horses. Leedro (4) <u>has discover</u> that his horse has a sore tendon. He (5) <u>will be giving</u> the horse a few days' rest. Horses are very important to a rancher. If a cow (6) <u>has broke</u> away from the herd, the cowhand must go after it on horseback.

1. A will riding
   B will be riding
   C will rode
   D No mistake

2. F are puting
   G be putting
   H are putting
   J No mistake

3. A they
   B their
   C theys
   D No mistake

4. F have discover
   G has discovered
   H have discovered
   J No mistake

5. A will be give
   B will giving
   C will have giving
   D No mistake

6. F has broken
   G has breaked
   H has broked
   J No mistake

7.–11. For items 1, 2, 4, 5, and 6, write the tense of the verb you chose as the correct answer.

CONTRACTIONS AND NEGATIVES

Skill Reminder

- A **contraction** is a shortened form of (usually) two words. An apostrophe takes the place of one or more letters that have been left out.

- **Negatives** are words that mean "no" or "not." Negatives include *no, not, never, nowhere, nothing, nobody, no one, neither, scarcely,* and *barely.*

- Use only one negative in a sentence.

Write each sentence, replacing the contraction with complete words.

1. You'll be surprised at the news.
2. We're quite excited.
3. They've flown an airplane.
4. That flight wasn't long.
5. The pilot hasn't called the newspapers.

Write each sentence, correcting any errors in the use of pronouns, contractions, or negatives.

6. Its a call from a reporter.
7. Weren't there no more calls?
8. Aren't there no photographs?
9. Your both heroes.
10. Wasnt there motor trouble?

CONTRACTIONS AND NEGATIVES

Write each sentence, replacing the underlined words with a contraction.

1. The plane <u>is not</u> too high.
2. Orville and Wilbur <u>are not</u> discouraged.
3. The flight <u>will not</u> begin for an hour.
4. I hope it <u>does not</u> rain.
5. <u>Have</u> they <u>not</u> flown before?
6. I <u>have not</u> been watching the sky closely.

Write each sentence correctly.

7. Haven't you never flown before?
8. The wind isn't scarcely blowing.
9. The plane never went nowhere.
10. Isn't you're brother a pilot?
11. Its a perfect day for flying.

CUMULATIVE REVIEW

Write the verb phrase used in each sentence. Then write whether it is *present progressive*, *past progressive*, or *future progressive*.

1. Orville is repairing the wing.

2. Wilbur was helping him.

3. The brothers were working carefully.

4. Will they be flying soon?

Write each sentence, replacing the underlined verb with the tense called for in parentheses.

5. The machine <u>starts</u> forward into the wind. (present perfect)

6. Orville <u>releases</u> the wire. (past perfect)

7. By lunchtime, the plane <u>lifts</u> up into the air. (future perfect)

Choose the correct version of each sentence. Write the correct letter. For items 10 and 11, there are two correct versions.

8. A The plane is moving, and its in flight.

   B The plane is moving, and it's in flight.

9. A You're in a good place to take a picture.

   B Your in a good place to take a picture.

10. A Did you never have a camera?

    B Didn't you never have a camera?

    C Didn't you ever have a camera?

11. A That plane didn't go nowhere.

    B That plane went nowhere.

    C That plane didn't go anywhere.

ADVERBS

Write the adverb used in each sentence. Write whether it describes *how, when, where, how often,* or *to what extent.*

1. The astronaut examined the screen carefully.

2. Soon a chart appeared.

3. An arrow blinked repeatedly.

4. She used the computer mouse to move the arrow down.

Write each adverb and the word it modifies. Then write whether the modified word is a *verb*, an *adjective*, or an *adverb*.

5. Astronauts practice tasks repeatedly.

6. Their spacesuits are extremely bulky.

7. Airplanes dive very quickly, producing a moment of weightlessness.

ADVERBS

Write each sentence, using an adverb from the box that provides the information in parentheses

not	everywhere	easily

1. Students can (how) learn about space science.
2. It is (to what extent) difficult to find a space museum or a space camp.
3. NASA sends educational materials to schools (where).

Write the paragraph, replacing each numbered space with an adverb from the box below.

ever	together	recently	quite	regularly	there	possibly

Have you (4) been to space camp? Some friends of mine (5) spent some time at one. Campers learn many things (6). These skills are (7) useful on space missions. Astronauts might (8) have to survive in the open ocean. Everyone works (9) in teams at a space camp. Students (10) apply to attend the space camps in California, South Carolina, and Alabama.

Write each sentence, completing it with an adverb of your choice.

11. Space scientists ____ study Earth's environment.
12. Weather patterns can be seen ____ from a space shuttle.
13. Astronauts become ____ familiar with the feeling of weightlessness.
14. Simulated spaceflights can be ____ realistic.

CUMULATIVE REVIEW

Write the letter of each correct sentence.

1. A   The rocket has lifted off, and its almost out of sight.

    B   The rocket has lifted off, and it's almost out of sight.

2. A   The spectators didn't go anywhere until it was over.

    B   The spectators didn't go nowhere until it was over.

3. A   Nothing like this has ever been seen before.

    B   Nothing like this has never been seen before.

4. A   I hope you brought you're camera.

    B   I hope you brought your camera.

Write the verb phrase used in each sentence. Write whether it is *present progressive, past progressive,* or *future progressive.*

5. The crew are planning many experiments.

6. Some of them were checking their instruments.

7. Others will be monitoring their body conditions.

Write each sentence, using the adverb from the box that describes the word in parentheses.

suddenly   soon   instantly

8. In 1986 the shuttle *Challenger* (how) exploded after blastoff.

9. All seven crew members died (when) in the blast.

10. (When) afterward their parents set up a space education program in their honor.

COMPARING WITH ADVERBS

- Use the **positive** form of an adverb when no comparison is being made.

- Use the **comparative** form to compare one action with one other action. To form the comparative of most short adverbs, add *er.* For other adverbs, especially those ending in *ly,* use *more.*

- Use the **superlative** form to compare one action with two or more other actions. To form the superlative of most short adverbs, add *est.* For other adverbs, especially those ending in *ly,* use *most.*

- *Less* and *least* are also used to form comparatives and superlatives. They may be used with short or long **adverbs**, and they indicate that the words are being compared negatively: *Jupiter orbits the sun less rapidly than Earth does,* meaning "not as rapidly."

- *Well* and *badly* have special forms of comparing.

Write the adverb used in each sentence. Then write whether it is in *positive, comparative,* or *superlative* form.

1. **Earth orbits the sun more rapidly than Jupiter does.**

2. **The rings of Saturn showed up less clearly through a telescope than on the screen.**

3. **Scientists could see Jupiter clearly with the *Voyagers.***

4. **Of all Jupiter's spots, the Great Red Spot swirls most violently.**

5. **The moons were seen better than ever before.**

6. **_Voyager 2_ was launched earlier than *Voyager 1*.**

COMPARING WITH ADVERBS

Draw the chart, filling in each empty space with the correct form of the adverb.

	POSITIVE	COMPARATIVE	SUPERLATIVE
1.	rapidly		
2.		better	
3.		more brightly	
4.	soon		
5.			most frequently
6.	badly		
7.			earliest
8.	high		
9.	energetically		
10.		more heavily	

Write each sentence, using the correct comparing form of the adverb in parentheses.

11. Details appear (clearly) in the *Voyager* photos than in telescope images.

12. Of all Jupiter's moons, Europa shines (brightly).

13. The spacecraft went through the asteroid belt (easily) than anyone had thought it would.

14. If an asteroid had hit Mimas (hard) than it did, that moon would have split apart.

15. Which craft will travel (long), *Voyager 1* or *Voyager 2*?

CUMULATIVE REVIEW

Write the adverb or adverbs used in each sentence. Then write whether the adverb modifies a *verb,* an *adjective,* or an *adverb.*

1. The satellite performed flawlessly.
2. The eruptions from the volcano were quite violent.
3. The lava flowed everywhere.
4. It cooled very quickly.

Write each sentence, correcting any errors in the use of pronouns, contractions, or negatives.

5. Its been several months since the liftoff.
6. We aren't never going to forget that sight.
7. Are youre parents following the journey, too?

Write each sentence, using the correct adverb and form in parentheses.

8. We saw the planets (distinctly; comparative) than ever before.
9. Of all the things we tried to see, we could distinguish the rings of Saturn (well; superlative).
10. We could not see Jupiter's Great Red Spot (clearly; positive).

PREPOSITIONAL PHRASES

Write the complete prepositional phrase. Then write the preposition and its object.

1. You can send an e-mail message to me.
2. I have an address on the Internet.
3. You can send a message anywhere in the world.
4. Any computer connected to the Internet can read your address.
5. Just type your address, the address of the person, and the message.
6. The subject line describes the message in a few words.

Write each sentence, using an appropriate preposition.

7. The Internet breaks your message ____ information bits.
8. These bits ____ information are sent individually.
9. Each bit contains the address ____ its destination.
10. Your address goes right along ____ every bit.

PREPOSITIONAL PHRASES

Write each sentence, adding a prepositional phrase. Use the word or words in parentheses in the phrase.

1. Have you ever sent e-mail? (friend)
2. If you ever do, you'll have to get acquainted. (Netiquette)
3. Don't use boldface type or underlining. (messages)
4. Messages are sometimes unreadable. (boldface type)
5. A sentence typed looks as if you shouted it. (capital letters)
6. People think that using only capital letters is very rude. (sender)
7. Only use capital letters. (emphasis)
8. If you get "flamed," you get a lot. (angry messages)

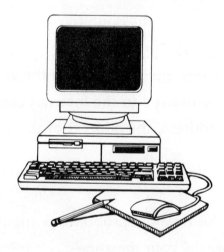

CUMULATIVE REVIEW

Write the adverb used in each sentence. Then write whether it is *positive*, *comparative*, or *superlative* in form.

1. You can learn to send e-mail more easily than you might think.
2. The message gets to its destination immediately.
3. People most frequently complain about the amount of mail.

Write the adverb used in each sentence. Then write whether it describes *how, when, where,* or *how often.*

4. Most people check their e-mail daily.
5. You can surf the Internet quickly.
6. Some people like to surf the Internet late in the evening.
7. People can surf databases in Europe and get information there.

Write each sentence, adding a prepositional phrase that makes sense.

8. There is a lot of information.
9. You may need to know the address first.
10. I sent an e-mail.

ADJECTIVE AND ADVERB PHRASES

- A prepositional phrase that modifies, or describes, a noun or a pronoun is an **adjective phrase**. Adjective phrases tell *what kind, which one,* or *how many.*

- A prepositional phrase that modifies, or describes, a verb, an adjective, or an adverb is an **adverb phrase**. Adverb phrases tell *how, when, where, how often,* or *to what extent.*

Write the adjective phrase used in each sentence. Then write the word the phrase modifies and whether the phrase describes *what kind, which one,* or *how many.*

1. Teachers asked questions about the lessons.

2. Regular teachers are computers with interactive programs.

3. The mind of each student is different.

4. The programs in the machines adjust their lessons.

5. The information about old schools fascinated Margie.

6. Margie imagined children from the whole neighborhood learning together.

Write the adverb phrase used in each sentence. Then write the word the phrase modifies and whether the phrase describes *how, when, where, how often,* or *to what extent.*

7. Teachers taught from books then.

8. Margie looked over Tommy's shoulder.

9. Today, lessons are shown on a big screen.

10. The machine scored tests in a few seconds.

ADJECTIVE AND ADVERB PHRASES

Combine each pair of sentences into one sentence that includes the underlined adjective phrase.

Example: Margie studies lessons. The lessons are <u>in geography</u>.

Margie studies lessons in geography.

1. The pages are put here. The pages are <u>of homework</u>.
2. This slot takes the pages. The slot is <u>in the machine</u>.
3. Margie's scores were getting worse. Her scores were <u>on tests</u>.
4. Margie was having trouble. The trouble was <u>with geography</u>.

Combine each pair of sentences into one sentence that includes the underlined adverb phrase.

5. Each child can learn. This occurs <u>at a different pace</u> for each child.
6. Margie read. The reading was <u>about the old schools</u>.
7. The inspector repaired the mechanical teacher. The repair was finished <u>in a short time</u>.
8. Tommy carried the book. It was <u>under his arm</u>.

CUMULATIVE REVIEW

Read the paragraph. Then choose the word or group of words that best fits each numbered space.

   The book in the attic was the strangest thing Tommy had ever seen. He examined it **(1)**. Its pages had words **(2)**. He showed the book to Margie. She looked at it very **(3)**. She was glad Tommy had showed it **(4)**. She **(5)** seen a book like it before.

1. A   most close

   B   most closely

   C   closely

   D   close

2. F   on them

   G   on they

   H   on it

   J   on

3. A   much curiously

   B   more curious

   C   most curious

   D   curiously

4. F   to her

   G   to hers

   H   to she

   J   to it

5. A   hadn't ever

   B   had never

   C   had not nowhere

   D   hadn't not

Additional Practice

ADDITIONAL PRACTICE

Sentences

A. Write whether each group of words is a *sentence* or *not a sentence*.

Example:

A light danced in the sky.
Sentence

1. Moved rapidly.
2. It hovered quite close to the ground.
3. Making no noise at all.
4. We heard nothing.
5. The bottom of the object was lit brightly.
6. The object flew straight up and away.

B. Write whether each sentence is *declarative* or *interrogative*. Then write the sentence correctly.

Example:

What is the shape of the object
Interrogative—What is the shape of the object?

7. There have been many reports of UFOs
8. Have you ever had such an experience
9. No, I haven't
10. I have read some of the reports, though
11. Has anyone seen the inside of a flying saucer

12. What did it look like

13. Were there instrument panels

14. There are no pictures available

15. One person described her experience

16. Was it printed in any magazine

C. Write whether each sentence is *exclamatory* or *imperative*. Then write the sentence correctly.

Example:

What an amazing photograph that is
exclamatory—What an amazing photograph that is!

17. Look carefully at that photograph

18. What an unusual background it has

19. Observe the shape of the object

20. What a sweeping view of the sky this is

21. Give me that magnifying glass

22. How amazing the new technology is

23. Imagine yourself on a journey to a faraway planet

24. Describe your feelings

25. How lonely space must be

ADDITIONAL PRACTICE

Complete and Simple Subjects

On your paper, make two columns. In the first column, write the complete subject of each sentence. In the second column, write the simple subject of each sentence.

Example:

Several members of the crew were sewing costumes.

Complete Subject	Simple Subject
Several members of the crew	*members*

1. Ann was working in the costume room.
2. Many costumes were still unfinished.
3. Other outfits needed alterations.
4. Four students joined the costume crew.
5. A new costume was needed right away.
6. The velvet fabric was a challenge to cut.
7. Ann cut the cloth according to the pattern.
8. The pieces of velvet fit together well.

Writing Application Imagine that your class is putting on a play based on a selection you have just read. Write a paragraph telling which part you would like to play, and why. Underline each complete subject once and each simple subject twice.

9.   A number of students were building sets.

10. The director of the play entered the costume room.

11. His name was Mr. Frank Farwell.

12. A full script of the play was in his hand.

13. He hurried over to Ann.

14. The girl with the leading role had become ill.

15. Ann had also auditioned for the part.

16. She had almost won the role.

17. Mr. Farwell had chosen Ann as the replacement.

18. Ann's character would speak many lines.

19. Ann's brother helped her with her lines.

20. Only one week of rehearsals remained.

21. The day of the last dress rehearsal finally arrived.

22. The rehearsal lasted a long time.

23. The members of the cast were nervous on opening night.

24. The big maroon curtain opened.

25. Ann's friends congratulated her on her success.

ADDITIONAL PRACTICE

Complete and Simple Predicates

On your paper, make two columns. In the first column, write the complete predicate of each sentence. In the second column, write the simple predicate of each sentence.

Example:

Ralph spaded the earth vigorously.

Complete Predicate	*Simple Predicate*
spaded the earth vigorously	*spaded*

1. He broke large lumps of dirt into smaller ones.
2. He raked the surface of the soil.
3. Ralph's father laid plants on the ground.
4. The two gardeners dug a separate hole for each plant.
5. Ralph heaped new soil around the roots of the plants.
6. A hose lay nearby on the walkway.
7. Ralph's sister Liz watered the plants generously.
8. Fertilizer would help the plants' growth.

9. Ralph watered the plants every other day.

10. He also pulled weeds from the garden.

11. Green leaves sprouted soon on all the plants.

12. The stalks grew taller and taller.

13. All of Ralph's plants were growing well.

14. One healthy plant was smaller than the others.

15. That plant needed special care.

16. Ralph gave the little plant daily attention.

17. The other plants dwarfed the small one.

18. Ralph's father called the little plant the "runt" of the garden.

19. The little plant looked healthy.

20. None of the plants had produced any flowers.

21. Some plants would not bloom at all.

22. Ralph went out to the garden early one morning.

23. He inspected each plant.

24. Ralph called to the other members of the family.

25. The littlest plant of all had three lovely flowers!

ADDITIONAL PRACTICE

Compound Subjects and Predicates

Write whether each sentence has a *compound subject* or a *compound predicate.* Then write the simple subjects in each compound subject and the simple predicates in each compound predicate.

Example:

Felicia opened the back door of the house and sat on the back steps.
compound predicate—opened, sat

1. Felicia and Alfio were unhappy.

2. Alfio came out of the house and joined Felicia.

3. The young girl and her twin brother would have a birthday soon.

4. They enjoyed life on the farm but were somewhat lonely.

5. Their mother and father had said nothing about the twins' birthday.

6. Alfio and Felicia had not expressed anything directly to their parents.

7. The twins' parents understood the problem and had discussed it.

8. The children's friends lived several miles away and rarely visited.

9. Felicia's parents sometimes talked with each other but kept their voices soft.

10. Felicia and Alfio woke up early on the morning of their birthday.

11. They rushed down the stairs and ran into the kitchen.

12. Mother was fixing breakfast and wished them a happy birthday.

13. The two children ate and then dressed.

14. Father came into the house but said nothing.

15. Then he took them outside and walked them to the barn.

16. Mother and Father smiled at each other.

17. Father went into the barn and finally emerged with a young llama.

18. The llama was their birthday present and soon became everyone's favorite pet.

ADDITIONAL PRACTICE
Simple and Compound Sentences

Identify each sentence as a *simple sentence* or a *compound sentence.*

Example:

Llamas do not look like camels, but they are related to them.
compound sentence

1. A llama is not a wild animal.

2. Llamas are quite gentle, and people often make pets of them.

3. The llama is native to South America.

4. Herds of llamas are kept by the native people of the mountains of Peru and Bolivia.

5. Llamas climb easily over rocky terrain and make good pack animals in the mountains.

6. A llama has two toes on each foot, and this physical trait gives it unusual climbing ability.

7. They have adapted to places between 10,000 and 17,000 feet above sea level.

8. A llama is not carnivorous and prefers grasses and leaves as food.

9. A llama has a cleft, or divided, upper lip, and it can nibble at all sorts of things easily.

10. These animals are tamer than domesticated farm animals.

11. They enjoy humans as company, and they are quite affectionate.

12. They have no natural defense feature such as horns.

13. An angry llama will pull its ears back and spit.

14. Ruth Janette Ruck has a pet llama and has written a book about her experiences.

15. The book is entertaining and informative, and interested people should read it.

16. Some experts on llamas do not have all their facts correct.

17. Ruck talked to one expert, and he told her something interesting.

18. The llama lacks speech organs and is mute.

19. Ruck herself discovered otherwise.

20. Llamas emit a humming sound, and you can hear it.

Writing Application What would happen if a llama visited your school? Write several simple and compound sentences about the event. See who comes up with the wildest story!

ADDITIONAL PRACTICE

Clauses and Phrases

A. On your paper, make two columns. In the first column, list the underlined phrases from these sentences. In the second column, list the underlined clauses.

Example:

Frank stared at the dirty walls as he stirred the paint.

Phrase	*Clause*
at the dirty walls	*as he stirred the paint*

1. Before he could paint them, he had to wash the walls of the dining room.

2. Frank filled a bucket with washing compound and water.

3. Frank scrubbed hard for two hours, and at last the walls were free of dirt.

4. When Frank finished, he looked at each wall.

5. Because the paint on one wall was thin, Frank noticed something beneath the surface.

6. With a scraper, he peeled some paint from one part of the wall.

7. A painting was revealed; perhaps it was an old mural.

8. After he called his father, Frank scraped more paint from the bottom of the wall.

9. Frank continued with the difficult job until all the paint had been scraped away.

Independent and Dependent Clauses

B. Write whether the underlined group of words in each sentence is an *independent clause* or a *dependent clause.* If it is a dependent clause, identify the *subordinating conjunction* that connects it to the rest of the sentence.

Example:

<u>All artists need inspiration for their work,</u> and many of them gain such inspiration from the culture of their native land.
independent clause

10. <u>Diego Rivera was one of the greatest painters and muralists of Mexico.</u>

11. <u>Because he loved Mexico,</u> his works often portray the culture and history of that country.

12. One of his paintings reflects the time <u>before the Spanish conquered Mexico.</u>

13. <u>That painting shows the Zapotec Indians making gold jewelry.</u>

14. <u>Although Rivera did some of his most famous murals in Mexico City,</u> several of his works were painted in the United States.

15. If you want to see one of Rivera's best works, <u>visit the Detroit Institute of Arts.</u>

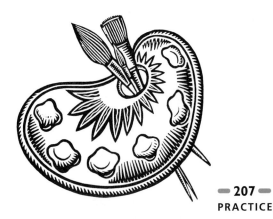

ADDITIONAL PRACTICE

Complex Sentences

Tell whether each sentence is a *simple sentence,* a *compound sentence,* or a *complex sentence.*

Example:

Although no one is sure why, the number of salmon in the Pacific Northwest has decreased alarmingly.
complex sentence

1. The salmon has been an endangered animal for many years.

2. Logging caused a problem for the spotted owl, but the causes of the salmon problem are more complex.

3. Because a number of species of salmon are threatened, solutions can cost a great deal.

4. Where salmon spawn each year in the upper Columbia River basin, the fish used to number anywhere from 10 million to 16 million.

5. That number decreased to about 2,500,000, and it may decrease further.

6. As some scientists calculate, perhaps nineteen types of salmon may already be extinct.

7. More than one-third of the entire habitat of the salmon has been destroyed.

8. The chinook salmon is a greatly endangered species, but the sockeye and the coho are also in trouble.

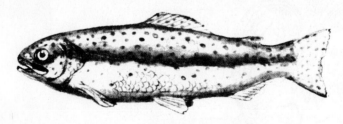

9. Another endangered fish is the steelhead trout.

10. Irrigation runoff water contains dangerous chemicals, and dams have reduced the water flow to rivers.

11. These two factors have damaged the rivers of the Northwest, but overfishing and building developments have also contributed.

12. Because dams block the water flow, the young salmon are not carried out to sea on strong currents of fresh water.

13. Even more fish have died because of a seven-year drought.

14. Fish born in human-made hatcheries do not swim upstream well since they do not have the energy of wild salmon.

15. Emergency rulings from the government may be necessary before real help for the salmon is possible.

Writing Application Most communities have special places where people can enjoy nature. Choose a place that has trees, water, or animals. Write at least three complex sentences about what you might see and hear there.

ADDITIONAL PRACTICE

Common and Proper Nouns

On your paper, make two columns. In the first column, list the common nouns in each sentence. In the second column, list the proper nouns.

Example:

Claude Monet first exhibited his paintings in Paris.

Common Nouns	*Proper Nouns*
paintings	*Claude Monet*
	Paris

1. Monet was the first painter of the school of painting called Impressionism.

2. The name of his new style came from a painting by Monet called *Impression: Sunrise.*

3. The movement began in nineteenth-century France.

4. Monet was joined by thirty-nine other artists.

5. Those painters included Pierre-Auguste Renoir, Edgar Degas, and Paul Cézanne.

6. The first exhibit of paintings by this group was in Paris in April 1874.

7. The Impressionists wanted to capture on canvas how the eye saw light.

8. These painters were concerned with the way objects reflect light.

9. Monet often painted from a boat on the river Seine.

10. Monet died on December 5, 1926.

Singular and Plural Nouns

On your paper, make two columns. Label one *Singular* and the other *Plural.* Write each noun in the correct column. Then write the other form.

Example:

baby

Singular

baby

Plural

babies

1. hero
2. ox
3. blueberries
4. women
5. blush
6. mouth
7. reef
8. canary
9. glitches
10. umbrellas
11. wells
12. vase
13. mosses
14. lance
15. mass
16. patch
17. video
18. mouse
19. gulch
20. cello
21. wishes
22. zipper
23. flash
24. cities
25. puppy

Writing Application Look around the classroom. List at least ten things you see. Then write the plural form of each noun, and use some of the plural nouns in sentences.

ADDITIONAL PRACTICE

Possessive Nouns

A. Identify which groups of words in these sentences you could replace with possessive nouns. Then rewrite each sentence, using a possessive noun.

Example:

The first mathematicians of the ancient world were the Egyptians in Africa.
The ancient world's first mathematicians were the Egyptians in Africa.

1. The knowledge of mathematics and science of the ancient Egyptians was put to practical use.

2. The computation system of the Egyptians was used to find areas and volumes.

3. The standard unit of length of the surveyors was the *cubit,* the length of the forearm of a person.

4. The skill of the mathematicians in geometry was used in the construction of the pyramids.

5. The knowledge of the Egyptians of astronomy was also quite remarkable.

6. The observations of the astronomers led them to distinguish the stars from the planets.

7. Alexandria, Egypt, was the home of the most famous library of the ancient world.

8. The scroll collection of the Alexandrian Library was the largest of the ancient world.

B. Write the singular possessive form of each noun.

Example:

week
week's

9. country
10. thief
11. Robert Frost
12. sculptor
13. minute
14. weaver

15. Samuel Clemens
16. wolf
17. nurse
18. King Henry
19. moment
20. secretary

C. Write the plural possessive form of each noun.

Example:

women
women's

21. masters
22. workers
23. hours
24. oxen
25. spies
26. buffaloes

27. surgeons
28. (the) Toronto Blue Jays
29. sheep
30. secretaries

ADDITIONAL PRACTICE

Pronouns

A. List the personal pronouns in these sentences. Write the number and gender of each one.

Example:

When Christopher Columbus died in 1506, he was an unhappy man.
he; singular, masculine

1. Columbus explored the islands he had found in the West Indies.

2. They were referred to as "the New World."

3. Queen Isabella gave her support to the journey.

4. Columbus was a great seaman, but his skills as a colonizer were poor.

5. He left a group of men at Hispaniola, but all of them were killed.

B. Identify each pronoun in the following sentences. Write whether the pronoun is a *subject, object,* or *reflexive pronoun.*

Example:

Monica did not injure herself.
herself; reflexive

6. Monica told herself that she must drive slowly.

7. Monica's younger sister and brother were with her.

Writing Application Choose a historical figure from your social studies textbook or another book you have read. Write a paragraph about why that person was important. Underline the pronouns you use.

8. Brother Bob said that he was hungry.

9. The children amused themselves by singing.

10. Cars pulled off the highway because it was icy.

11. Monica drove slowly, but she still lost control.

12. For a moment she found herself helpless.

13. Then she maneuvered the car and stopped it.

C. Write the antecedent of each underlined pronoun.

Example:

Julia Ward Howe is remembered for the words <u>she</u> wrote for "The Battle Hymn of the Republic."
Julia Ward Howe

14. "John Brown's Body" was a popular song with Union soldiers as <u>they</u> marched in the Civil War.

15. Howe wrote <u>her</u> words to be sung to that melody.

16. Howe's song was published in a magazine, but <u>she</u> was not named as the author.

17. Many famous poets voiced <u>their</u> praise for the lyrics.

18. <u>Her</u> words remained popular with soldiers.

19. <u>They</u> sang <u>them</u> during World War I.

ADDITIONAL PRACTICE

Pronouns

Write the possessive pronoun that is needed to complete
each sentence.

Example:

Residents of St. Petersburg, Russia, are proud of ____ city.
their

1. We traveled to St. Petersburg to visit ____ friends.

2. Boris took us to see some of the most beautiful sights
   in ____ native city.

3. I made sure I had brought ____ camera along.

4. Marie and I, together with ____ friends, took a boat
   down the canals of the city.

5. Boris pointed out palaces where some of Russia's great
   rulers had made ____ homes.

6. At night the sun still sheds ____ light on the city.

7. On nights at home, Russians love to make tea; it is
   ____ favorite beverage.

8. Tea and apple cake is a favorite late-night snack of
   ____.

9. St. Petersburg is full of flea markets where merchants show off ____ wares.

10. The traders set up ____ stalls along Nevsky Prospekt.

11. Marie invited us on a trip to one of ____ favorite islands.

12. This place has a charm all ____ own.

13. During World War II, the citizens of St. Petersburg endured a 900-day siege of ____ city by the Germans.

14. We saw a man with a ribbon on ____ coat showing that he was a veteran of that siege.

15. People who suffered through that period wear ____ ribbons proudly.

16. Snow, ice, hunger, and disease took ____ toll among the brave residents of St. Petersburg.

17. ____ name at the time was Leningrad, after Lenin, a leader of the revolution of 1917.

Writing Application On the Internet, research the history of your city or state. Choose one time period, and write a brief research report about it. Be sure to use possessive pronouns correctly.

ADDITIONAL PRACTICE

Adjectives and Articles

A. On your paper, make two columns. In the first column, list the adjectives and articles in each sentence. In the second column, write the word that each adjective or article describes.

Example:

Cheetahs are large cats.

Adjective/Article	*Word Described*
large	*cats*

1. Cheetahs live on the grassy plains of Africa.

2. An adult cheetah can run at a top speed of 70 miles per hour.

3. Cheetahs live on the broad grasslands of the Serengeti.

4. They are found in various parts of India as well as in Africa.

5. The cheetah has a slender body.

6. The long legs of a cheetah cover ground quickly.

7. The coat is brownish yellow with black spots.

8. The hair on the underbelly is white.

9. The lordly lion is a daytime predator, but the cheetah is a nocturnal hunter.

10. The large cats are magnificent creatures.

B. List the proper adjectives in these sentences.

Example:

These Egyptian mummies are quite old.
Egyptian

11. The Alexandrian Library held the largest collection of scrolls in the ancient world.

12. Alexandria was the center of Mediterranean culture.

13. The Arabs moved the Egyptian capital from Alexandria to Cairo in the seventh century A.D.

14. Alexandria became part of the Turkish Empire.

15. The city was an important naval base for British ships during both world wars.

C. Rewrite each sentence, using the demonstrative adjective correctly.

Example:

Where is Madagascar on these map?
Where is Madagascar on this map?

16. Those island is off the coast of Mozambique.

17. This lemurs make their home on Madagascar.

18. That animals can be found nowhere else.

19. Those rain forest is being cut down.

20. These destruction is ruining many habitats.

ADDITIONAL PRACTICE

Comparing with Adjectives: Positive, Comparative, and Superlative Forms

A. Write the comparative and superlative forms of these adjectives.

Example:

hot
hotter, hottest

1. salty
2. odd
3. beautiful
4. dim
5. mischievous

6. brave
7. muddy
8. confident
9. simple
10. rosy

B. Write the form of the adjective in parentheses ( ) that correctly completes the sentence.

Example:

Which of the ten cruise ships has the (low) cost of all?
lowest

11. Which cruise takes the (long) time of all?
12. Is this ship (long) than that one?
13. Which of the cruises has the (tasty) food?
14. A (small) ship might be more fun than a (larger) one.

15. Once, only the (wealthy) people of all could afford cruises.

16. Now, prices are (cheap) and (affordable) than they once were.

17. Cruises are (popular) than ever before.

18. Ads for cruises in newspapers and on TV are (common) than they once were.

19. The cost for a luxury cruise is (great) than for any other.

20. Does this cruise have a (high) cost than that cruise?

C. Write the form of the adjective in parentheses ( ) that correctly completes the sentence.

Example:

The (good) thing to do on a trip is to travel light.
best

21. Less baggage is (good) than (much) baggage.

22. Of these two brochures, this one is (bad).

23. There are (much) pictures than words.

24. I was sick on the first day, but now I feel (well).

25. The cruise with the (little) cost of all is to Aruba.

ADDITIONAL PRACTICE

Action and Linking Verbs

On your paper, make two columns. In the first column, list the verb or verbs in each sentence. In the second column, write whether the verb is an *action verb* or a *linking verb*.

Example:

I remember the drive vividly.

Verb	*Action/Linking*
Remember	*action*

1. To those from warm climates, snow seems foreign.
2. We drove from Tucson to the Grand Canyon.
3. You literally go from one type of weather to the other.
4. The canyon is high above sea level.
5. Snow falls heavily there in winter.
6. In Tucson, temperatures are quite warm all year.
7. Arizona is definitely a world full of contrasts.

8. You see three different cultures everywhere.

9. The cultures are Anglo-American, Spanish, and Native American.

10. I recall the trip from Phoenix to Flagstaff.

11. I saw some of the most beautiful scenery.

12. We traveled from Prescott up to Sedona.

13. One scenic drive is the 16-mile road through Oak Creek Canyon.

14. The road ascends steadily to Flagstaff.

15. Strange things happen in the air at the Grand Canyon.

16. Sometimes you see the opposite side of the canyon.

17. At the same time, fog obscures the interior of the canyon.

18. At the bottom of the canyon flows the Colorado River.

19. There are many amazing sights nearby.

20. The Petrified Forest and the Painted Desert are memorable.

21. Petrified wood is wood that has turned to stone.

22. Guards protect petrified wood in the park from thieves.

23. Petrified wood has become a popular souvenir.

24. A meteor once hit near Winslow, Arizona, and created a crater.

25. Meteor Crater is 4,150 feet in diameter.

ADDITIONAL PRACTICE

Main and Helping Verbs

A. Write whether the underlined word in each sentence is a *main verb* or a *helping verb*.

Example:

The audience is <u>waiting</u> patiently.
main verb

1. The tiny curtain slowly <u>opens</u>.
2. Two figures <u>are</u> dancing into view.
3. The figures are <u>called</u> puppets.
4. Puppets can be <u>made</u> out of cloth and wood.
5. Our puppet theater <u>gives</u> three shows a year.
6. Each show <u>is</u> performed for four weekends.
7. New plays are <u>rehearsed</u> carefully.
8. I <u>have</u> become a puppeteer with the company.
9. I <u>am</u> memorizing lines and movements.
10. The new play was <u>written</u> in Spanish and English.
11. Sometimes our lines are <u>spoken</u> in English.
12. Sometimes audiences <u>have</u> asked for Spanish.
13. All the puppeteers <u>can</u> speak both languages.
14. We have been <u>doing</u> this for several years.
15. <u>Do</u> the audiences enjoy the shows?

B. Identify the verb phrase in each sentence. Then identify the main verb in each verb phrase.

Example:

Puppets are worked by hand from underneath.
are worked; worked

16. The puppet's body is made from a piece of cloth.

17. The body is fitted over the puppeteer's hand.

18. A thumb and forefinger can become the puppet's arms.

19. Other fingers are used in head movements.

20. Jim Henson is credited with creating a special kind of hand puppet for television.

21. His puppets are called Muppets.

22. Workers must use two hands for movements.

23. One hand is employed for the puppet's facial expressions.

24. Fingers can create smiles or frowns.

25. The other hand may move the hand or body.

Writing Application Think of an activity you have enjoyed since you were much younger. Write several sentences about the activity and why you have enjoyed it. Underline your main verbs once and your helping verbs twice.

ADDITIONAL PRACTICE

Transitive and Intransitive Verbs/Direct and Indirect Objects

A. On your paper, make four columns. List each verb or verb phrase in the first column. Write whether it is *transitive* or *intransitive* in the second column. If it is transitive, write its direct object in the third column. If there is also an indirect object, write it in the fourth column.

Example:

I gave the workers their money.

Verb	Type	Direct Object	Indirect Object
gave	transitive	money	workers

1. The workers had built a sturdy metal fence.
2. I inherited a cat from the former tenants.
3. Smith, the cat, sat quietly on the sofa.
4. I drove to the kennel for my two dogs, Jones and Koko.
5. The dogs would see Smith soon.
6. I offered the dogs treats.
7. I gave each dog a warning about politeness.
8. Then I entered the house with the two canines.
9. The cat bristled.
10. I gave the cat a hug.
11. The poodle, Koko, gave the cat a sniff.

12. Jones understood cats.

13. He sat quietly at a distance.

14. The cat surprised the dogs.

15. He gave each one a friendly kiss.

B. Expand each sentence so that it will have an indirect object as well as a direct object. Write the new sentences.

Example:

I brought treats.
I brought the animals treats.

16. When their guests arrived, the three pals gave a hearty welcome.

17. I sent holiday cards with pictures of the animals.

18. My friends asked questions about the first meeting.

19. A TV talk show host gave a spot on her program.

20. I told the facts.

21. An animal-food company sent boxes of free food.

22. A restaurant owner gave a free meal.

23. The animals brought a lot of public attention.

24. My neighbors bought new leashes.

25. The animals still give friendly greetings.

ADDITIONAL PRACTICE

Predicate Nominatives and Predicate Adjectives

A. Write whether each underlined word or group of words is a *predicate nominative* or a *predicate adjective.*

Example:

A Halloween pumpkin is a <u>jack-o'-lantern</u>.
predicate nominative

1. A pumpkin is really a <u>squash</u>.
2. In New England, "squash pie" is a favorite <u>dessert</u>.
3. The squash in the pie is <u>pumpkin</u>, of course.
4. Our family's pie maker is <u>Uncle Oscar</u>.
5. Oscar's pies are <u>delicious</u>.
6. As they come out of the oven, they look <u>scrumptious</u>.
7. Oscar's secret is the <u>seasoning</u>.
8. The pumpkin should not be too <u>large</u>.
9. Jack-o'-lanterns can be <u>big</u> or <u>small</u>.
10. A freshly baked pie is a <u>delight</u> to the eye.

B. Identify the predicate nominatives and predicate adjectives in these sentences.

Example:

That pumpkin looks strange.
strange; predicate adjective

11. It is quite heavy.
12. A pumpkin can become very large.
13. This one seems the largest.
14. It is the prizewinner.
15. At pumpkin time, the weather turns cold.
16. After the first frost, temperatures become mild again.
17. That warm period is a nice break from the cold temperatures.

C. Use each of these verbs in two sentences. In the first sentence, use the verb as an action verb. In the second sentence, use it as a linking verb.

18. turn
19. appear
20. feel

ADDITIONAL PRACTICE

Present, Past, and Future Tenses

A. Identify the verbs or verb phrases in these sentences. Write whether each verb is in the *present,* the *past,* or the *future* tense.

Example:

The Little League played a game today.
played; past

1. Teddy's team will bat first.
2. The visiting team always bats first.
3. Teddy's cousin Mary will pitch for his team
4. In the last game, she played first base.
5. Sometimes players change positions.
6. The coach gives everyone a chance at each position.
7. The visiting team scored one run in the first inning.
8. Our team fields well.
9. Teddy missed the first two pitches.
10. The ball sailed toward right field.
11. Teddy's home run ties the game.
12. Mary pitched seven innings.
13. Will the coach replace her?
14. The crowd cheered her as she walked off the field.
15. Our team will celebrate its third victory.

B. Write a sentence for each verb. Use the tense given in parentheses ( ).

Example:

watch (past)
We watched the game closely.

16. **shout (past)**

17. **surprise (future)**

18. **clap (present)**

19. **shrug (past)**

20. **use (future)**

21. **look (present)**

22. **ask (present)**

23. **wander (past)**

24. **explore (past)**

25. **attend (future)**

ADDITIONAL PRACTICE

Perfect Tenses

A. Identify the verb phrases in these sentences. Write whether each verb phrase is in the *present perfect,* the *past perfect,* or the *future perfect* tense.

Example:

Marla has purchased a new camera.
has purchased; present perfect

1. Marla has joined a camera club.

2. She has made photography her hobby.

3. The photo club had given her a prize.

4. By next month, Marla will have been a club member for three years.

5. The club has sponsored a contest every year for five years.

6. They have given more than fifty prizes so far.

7. By next year, they will have awarded more than sixty.

8. Marla had applied for club membership twice before.

9. Until this month, club members had needed a darkroom.

10. Members have applied part of their dues to the purchase of equipment.

Writing Application Brainstorm ideas for a funny dialogue between you and a classmate. Use perfect tenses in the dialogue. Share your dialogue by performing it.

B. Write each sentence using the correct perfect tense of the verb in parentheses ( ).

Example:

Your camera ____ repairs for some time. (need)
Your camera has needed repairs for some time.

11. I ____ a lot of film in the past two weeks. (use)

12. By the end of the month, I ____ more than $100 worth of film. (purchase)

13. Nila ____ many pictures of fall foliage this year. (snap)

14. She ____ pictures every year to magazines. (submit)

15. Recently, one magazine ____ her a job as a free-lance photographer. (promise)

16. Before that offer, she ____ her abilities. (doubt)

17. By next January, she ____ more than $5,000. (earn)

18. She ____ a new camera for herself. (purchase)

19. Nila ____ some of her techniques to me. (reveal)

20. Before I bought my new camera, I ____ only black-and-white film. (use)

ADDITIONAL PRACTICE

Principal Parts/Irregular Verbs

A. Write each sentence using the correct form of the verb or verbs in parentheses ( ).

Example:

We ____ to the circus last night. (go)
We went to the circus last night.

1. The circus ____ with a grand parade. (begin)

2. Every performer ____ a glittery costume. (wear)

3. I had ____ to the circus only once before. (be)

4. We had ____ refreshments before we ____ into the arena. (buy, go)

5. We like to ____ close to the top of the tent. (sit)

6. I could ____ the high-wire acts clearly. (see)

7. The acrobats ____ expertly through the air. (fly)

8. I had ____ there would ____ safety nets. (think, be)

9. Someone ____ the acrobat each time. (catch)

10. Have you ever ____ any acrobatic tricks? (do)

11. Our gym teacher has ____ us some tumbling skills. (teach)

12. I will never ____ those lessons. (forget)

13. I had not ___ the difficulty of such tricks. (understand)

14. We ___ the animals perform many feats. (see)

15. The work of the animal trainer ___ dangerous. (be)

B. Find the error or errors in each sentence. Write the sentence correctly.

Example:

One elephant hold a ball on the end of its trunk.
One elephant held a ball on the end of its trunk.

16. I have eat too many snacks.

17. Celia has came to the circus for five years.

18. Her aunt brung her this year.

19. Paolo has only went once before.

20. I had never saw a circus with three rings.

21. Paolo teared his shirt on a splinter.

22. I losed my hat in the crowd.

23. The clowns throwed candy into the crowd.

24. I catched two pieces.

25. When the acrobats flyed in the air, I nearly freezed with fear.

ADDITIONAL PRACTICE

Adverbs

Identify the adverb that describes each underlined word or
group of words. Then write whether the adverb tells *how,
when, where,* or *to what extent.*

Example:

The waves <u>washed</u> the shore gently.
gently; how

1. The sun <u>shone</u> down on the beach.
2. Children <u>splashed</u> noisily in the water.
3. Clouds <u>scudded</u> swiftly across the sky.
4. The serious surfers <u>arrived</u> first on the beach.
5. The largest crowds <u>appeared</u> later.
6. Lifeguards <u>watched</u> the swimmers carefully.
7. A strong undertow could be very <u>dangerous</u>.
8. One lifeguard <u>warned</u> a swimmer sternly.
9. Some swimmers seemed completely <u>unaware</u> of the danger.
10. Smart swimmers always <u>observe</u> the rules.
11. The children quickly <u>built</u> a castle in the sand.
12. A big wave <u>washed</u> away the castle.

Writing Application Describe a summer scene in your town
or city. Use adverbs to make your writing lively.

13. The young architects soon <u>constructed</u> another.

14. A very <u>wide</u> moat surrounded the new building.

15. The sand grew quite <u>hot</u> under the blazing sun.

16. People quickly <u>disappeared</u> under wide umbrellas.

17. A cool breeze <u>floated</u> overhead.

18. People <u>applied</u> sun block generously.

19. Some bathers wisely <u>had brought</u> picnic lunches.

20. The wind suddenly <u>became</u> cool.

21. Dark clouds completely <u>hid</u> the sun.

22. Swimmers rapidly <u>packed</u> their gear.

23. Some swimmers <u>huddled</u> quietly under their umbrellas.

24. Lifeguards shouted very <u>loudly</u> to those in the water.

25. Few people <u>remained</u> there on the beach.

ADDITIONAL PRACTICE

Comparing with Adverbs

A. Write the form of the adverb in parentheses ( ) that correctly completes each sentence.

Example:

Rain falls (heavily) in some regions than in others.
more heavily

1. In tropical climates, rainstorms occur (frequently) than in temperate zones.

2. Clouds fill with moisture (readily) over water than over land.

3. You can actually see the rain (easily) of all in places like Florida.

4. The wind direction shifts (noticeably) in the summer than in the winter.

5. In all its travels, the air soaks up moisture (rapidly) when it passes over the oceans.

Negatives

B. Write the word in parentheses ( ) that correctly completes the sentence. Avoid double negatives.

Example:

Don't (ever/never) cook rotten fish.
ever

6. Haven't you (never/ever) eaten fish?

7. There isn't (no/any) tastier food, I think.

8. You won't (never/ever) find shellfish along the surface of the sea.

9. There is (no/any) way they can move there.

10. Shellfish haven't (any/no) means of movement except along the sea bottom.

11. Some people won't (ever/never) eat lobster or crab meat.

12. Marvin said that he had (ever/never) eaten mackerel before.

13. He says nothing (ever/never) tasted so good.

14. When you live near the sea, buying fresh fish is (no/any) problem at all.

15. There isn't (anywhere/nowhere) better for someone who likes fish.

ADDITIONAL PRACTICE

Prepositions and Objects of the Preposition

A. The underlined word in each sentence is the object of a preposition. Write the preposition for each object.

Example:

The ship steamed slowly down the river.
down

1. Many passengers leaned over the railing.
2. The ship was bound for England.
3. People waved to the passengers.
4. A few people walked down the gangplank.
5. The ship would soon be sailing into the Atlantic Ocean.
6. The trip would last for five days.
7. For many people, this had been their first sea voyage.
8. That must have been a pleasant form of travel.

Writing Application Write a narrative about an experience on the water. Use prepositions in your narrative.

Prepositional Phrases

B. Write the prepositional phrase or phrases in each sentence. Identify the preposition.

Example:

The Chinese were the greatest sailors in history.
in history; in

9. The rudder, the single mast, the square sail, and the compass were all invented by the Chinese.

10. Can you imagine steering a boat without a rudder?

11. Sailors have always been guided by the stars in clear weather.

12. The use of the compass made navigation in cloudy weather possible.

13. The compass was first mentioned in a book written in 1117.

14. The compass was actually invented in China at a much earlier date.

15. The time of this invention was the fourth century B.C.

ADDITIONAL PRACTICE

Adjective Phrases

A. Write the sentences. Underline the adjective phrases.
Draw an arrow from each phrase to the word it modifies.

Example:

Three-fourths of the earth's surface is covered by water.
Three-fourths <u>of the earth's surface</u> is covered by water.

1. Two percent of that amount is frozen.

2. Rivers and lakes contain 1 percent of that water.

3. The oceans contain the rest of the water.

4. The four great oceans of the earth are the Atlantic, the Pacific, the Indian, and the Arctic.

5. The Pacific is the largest ocean on the earth.

6. The taste of ocean water is salty.

7. Dissolved salts make up 4 percent of ocean water.

8. That amount of salt makes ocean water really salty.

9. One mouthful of ocean water has more salt than a mouthful of potato chips.

10. Gulps of ocean water are quite unpleasant.

Writing Applicaiton Imagine a day at the beach. Write several sentences about what you smell, hear, see, and feel. Use adjective phrases to make your writing descriptive.

Adverb Phrases

B. Write the sentences. Underline the adverb phrases. Draw an arrow from the phrase to the word or words it modifies.

Example:

Oceanographers work beneath the ocean's surface.
Oceanographers work beneath the ocean's surface.

11. They descend in small diving ships.

12. Water pressure would crush some ships in a moment.

13. Specially designed ships can descend to 4,000-foot depths.

14. These vessels are designed for quick maneuvers.

15. Some of these ships carry scientists to the ocean floor.

16. Scientists view sunken ships with robotic cameras.

17. These robots can be maneuvered by remote control.

18. Television cameras send pictures to the surface.

19. Where water is not so deep, scientists are protected with diving suits.

20. Scientists can also descend in special underwater vehicles.

ADDITIONAL PRACTICE

Troublesome Words

A. Write the word in parentheses ( ) that correctly completes each sentence.

Example:

Tides (raise/rise) and fall each day.
rise

1. (Sit/Set) your beach bag on the car seat.
2. Soon we shall be (laying/lying) on the beach.
3. The temperature may (raise/rise) quite high today.
4. We should not (lay/lie) in the sun too long.
5. Let's (set/sit) down over there.
6. (Raise/Rise) your head so that I can put lotion on the back of your neck.
7. I'll (set/sit) the tube on the blanket.
8. We can (lie/lay) in the shade of those trees.
9. The sun (raised/rose) at 5:00 this morning.
10. It will not (set/sit) until early evening.

11. The whitecaps are (raising/rising) higher and higher.

12. Should we (lie/lay) down and let them roll over us?

13. I'd rather (set/sit) than (lie/lay) there.

14. I don't want to (raise/rise) my head and get a mouthful of salty water.

15. Well, then, let's (set/sit) in the shallow area.

16. Where did I (lie/lay) the water jug?

17. It's (laying/lying) right next to the picnic basket.

18. Invite your friends to (set/sit) with us.

19. (Set/Sit) the salt and pepper shakers over here.

20. (Rise/Raise) yourself a little more, and I will brush the sand off your back.

21. I guess I (lay/lied) on the sand too long today.

22. Let's swim a bit and then (lay/lie) down again.

23. I can't tell if the tide is (raising/rising) or falling.

24. It's falling because there's more beach to (set/sit) on now.

25. Oh, let's just (lie/lay) here and watch the waves.

ADDITIONAL PRACTICE

Punctuation: Commas with Introductory Words and Direct Address

A. Write each sentence, adding commas where they are needed.

Example:

Yes meadows are hard to find John.
Yes, meadows are hard to find, John.

1. Listen to me Sally.

2. Sally we are going to the Chicago Botanical Gardens today.

3. Well they have a new attraction.

4. No it's not a garden of exotic flowers.

5. Oh I thought I'd surprise you.

6. Okay it's a prairie garden.

7. The garden covers 15 acres Jed.

8. Yes humans have plowed up millions of acres of prairie for buildings.

9. No there are only about 2,300 acres of natural prairie left in Illinois now.

10. This human-made prairie is the botanists' gift to Illinois Sally.

Commas with Interrupters, Appositives, and Series

B. Write each sentence, adding commas where they are needed.

Example:

Roses paintbrush and clover are three plants you will find on the prairie.
Roses, paintbrush, and clover are three plants you will find on the prairie.

11. A prairie some people say is just a weed patch.

12. A prairie a kind of grassland is home to many kinds of plants and animals.

13. Animals feed on the leaves roots and stems of prairie plants.

14. Botanists according to a brochure transplanted 250,000 plants.

15. The total number of species in the garden I think is 250.

ADDITIONAL PRACTICE

Punctuation: Dialogue and Direct Quotations

Write each sentence. Add quotation marks where they are needed.

Example:

New York has a new program, Nancy said, for student ticket buyers.
"New York has a new program," Nancy said, "for student ticket buyers."

1. Yes, replied Mrs. Bensen. It's called High Five. Student tickets cost only five dollars.

2. All you need to do is show your school identification card, said Ben.

3. That sounds like a wonderful idea, Sam said.

4. Mrs. Bensen said, Some tickets you can buy right at box offices.

5. Others you can get at special ticket locations, she added.

6. Nancy remarked, You can also get tickets to dance programs and symphony concerts.

7. What a great idea! exclaimed Ralph.

8. The full price of a theater ticket is not cheap, said Sam.

9. Productions of Shakespeare's plays are available all over the city, I believe, said Mrs. Bensen.

10. Broadway shows are not available yet, but off-Broadway shows are, said Nancy.

11. Say, said Ralph, why don't we try to get something like that right here?

12. Well, said Mrs. Bensen, the city does have a cultural affairs department.

13. Let's write them a letter, said Nancy.

14. How about church choirs? asked Ben. They often give concerts.

15. Those are good suggestions, said Mrs. Bensen. Let's put them in our letter.

Writing Application Write a narrative about a person you admire. Use dialogue in your writing.

ADDITIONAL PRACTICE

Titles

Write correctly any titles used in the following sentences.

Example:

The magazine natural history is published by the American Museum of Natural History.

Natural History

1. One article listed in it is called our ecological past.

2. Did you see that movie about Dian Fossey called Gorillas in the Mist?

3. The planetarium has a holiday show called star of christmas.

4. The origami holiday tree is a popular museum tradition.

5. If you visit New York, try to see the phantom of the opera.

6. One show I'd enjoy seeing is guys and dolls.

7. It features the song luck be a lady tonight.

8. The musical cats is based on a book of poems by T. S. Eliot.

9. Eliot called his book old possum's book of practical cats.

10. One of the poems is called old deuteronomy.

11. Another poem is called macavity: the mystery cat.

12. The oldest cat of all sings the song memory.

13. A French play called cyrano de bergerac was turned into the musical cyrano.

14. Seussical is a musical based on stories written by Dr. Seuss.

15. Will anyone ever write a musical about the house at pooh corner?

Writing Application Brainstorm some silly titles of stories, musicals, songs, and books. Write each title correctly.

ADDITIONAL PRACTICE

Abbreviations

Write the correct abbreviation of each term. Use a dictionary, if necessary.

Example:

Maine
ME

1. pound
2. ounce
3. foot
4. yard
5. kilometer
6. milligram
7. liter
8. cubic centimeter
9. inch
10. quart
11. gallon
12. Florida
13. California
14. Virginia
15. United States of America

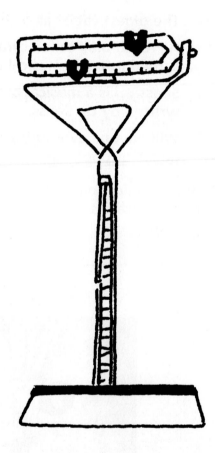

16. United States Military Academy
17. National Basketball Association
18. Michigan Boulevard
19. Rodeo Drive
20. Old Post Road
21. Fifth Avenue
22. National Collegiate Athletic Association
23. medical doctor
24. miles per hour
25. revolutions per minute
26. Fahrenheit
27. Celsius
28. October
29. February
30. September

E

F

G

H

I

J

L

M

N